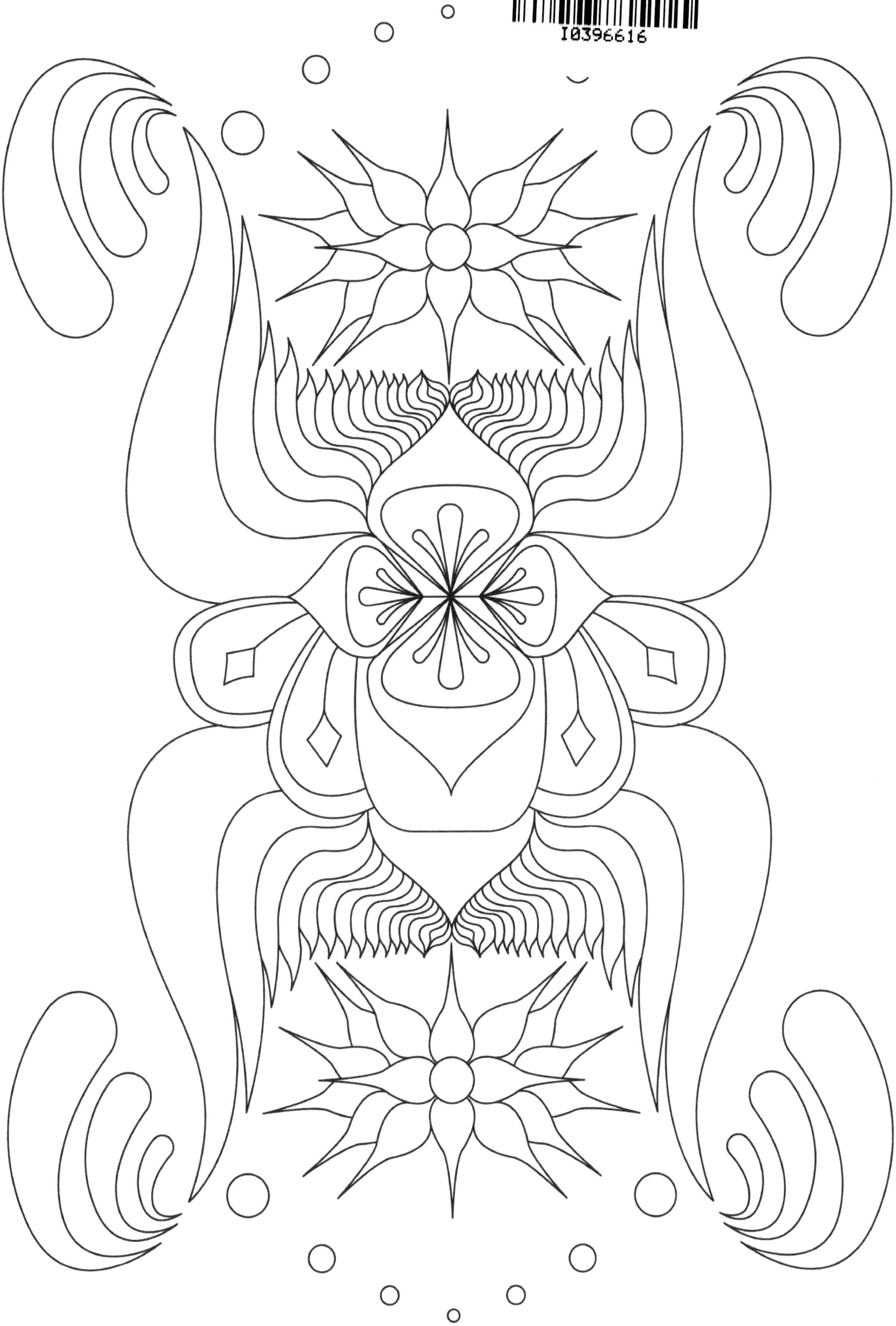

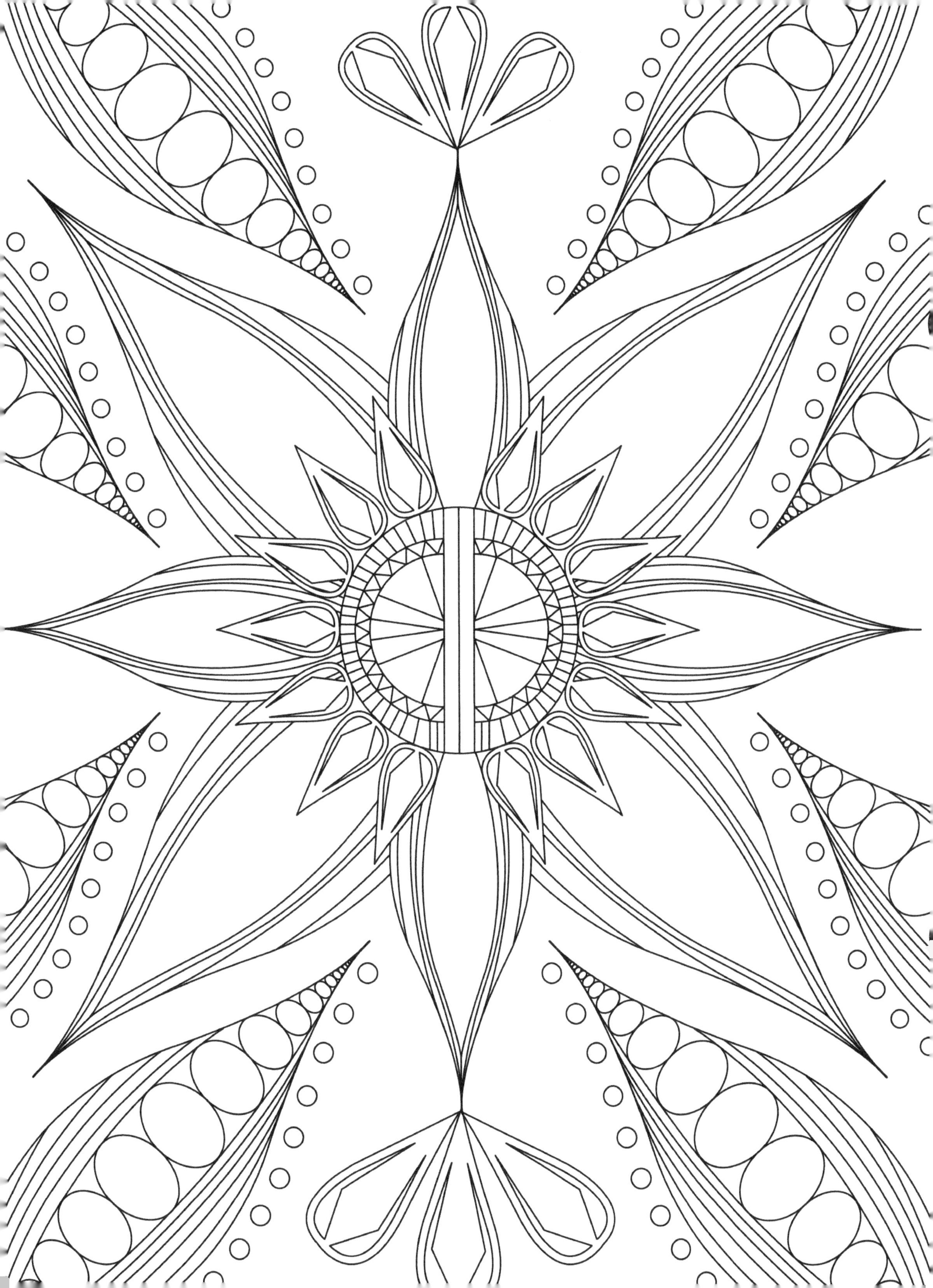

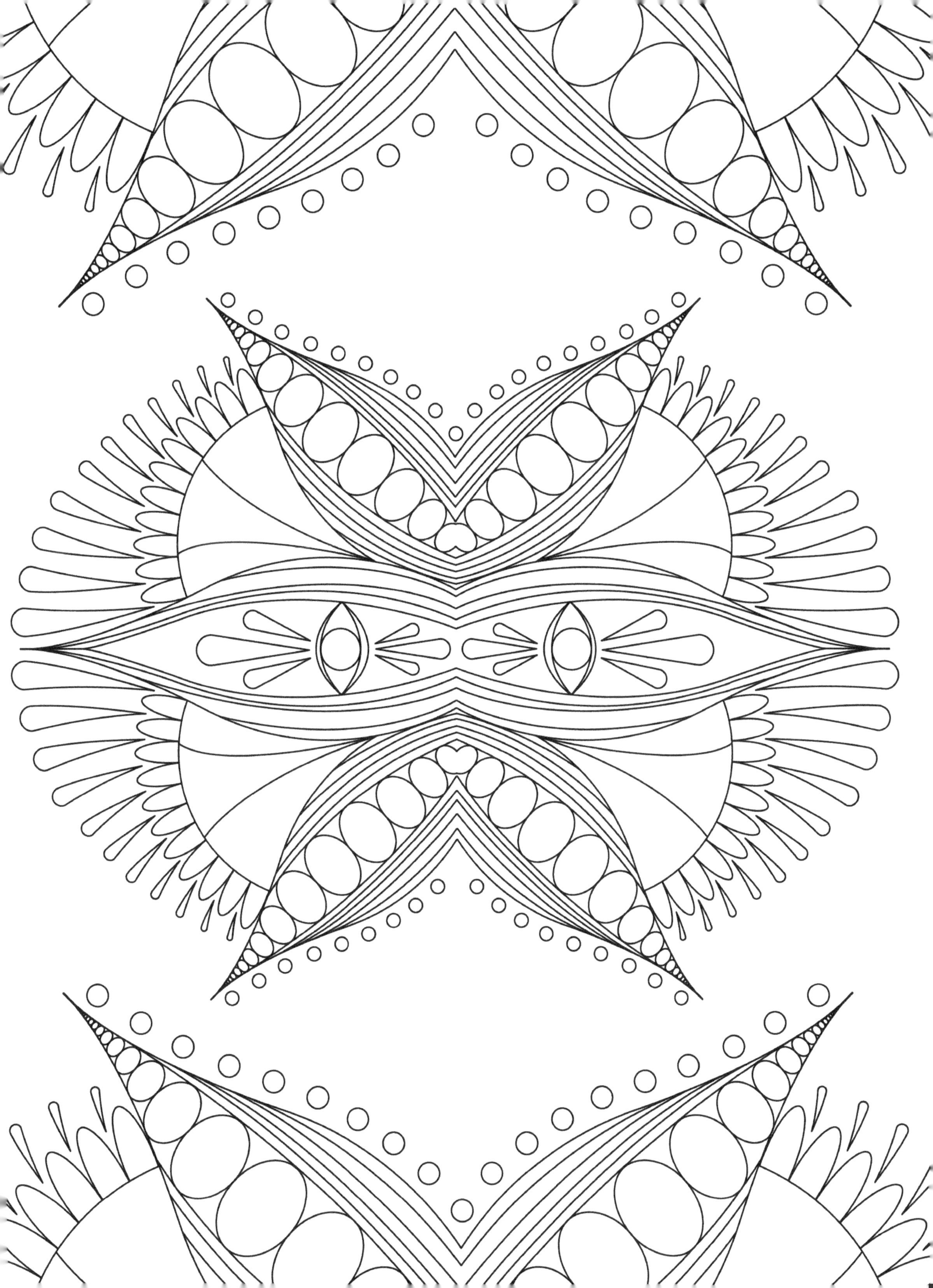

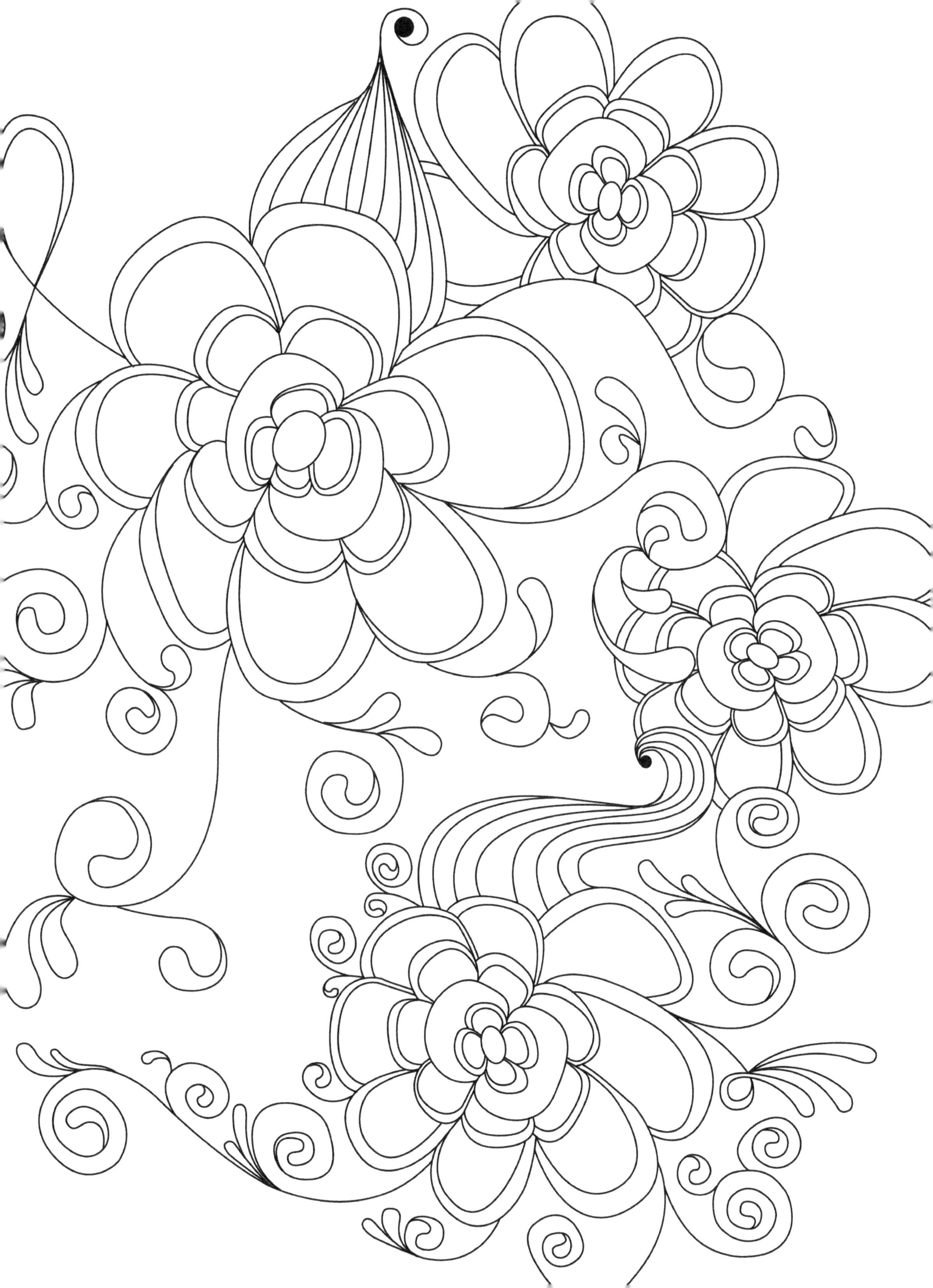

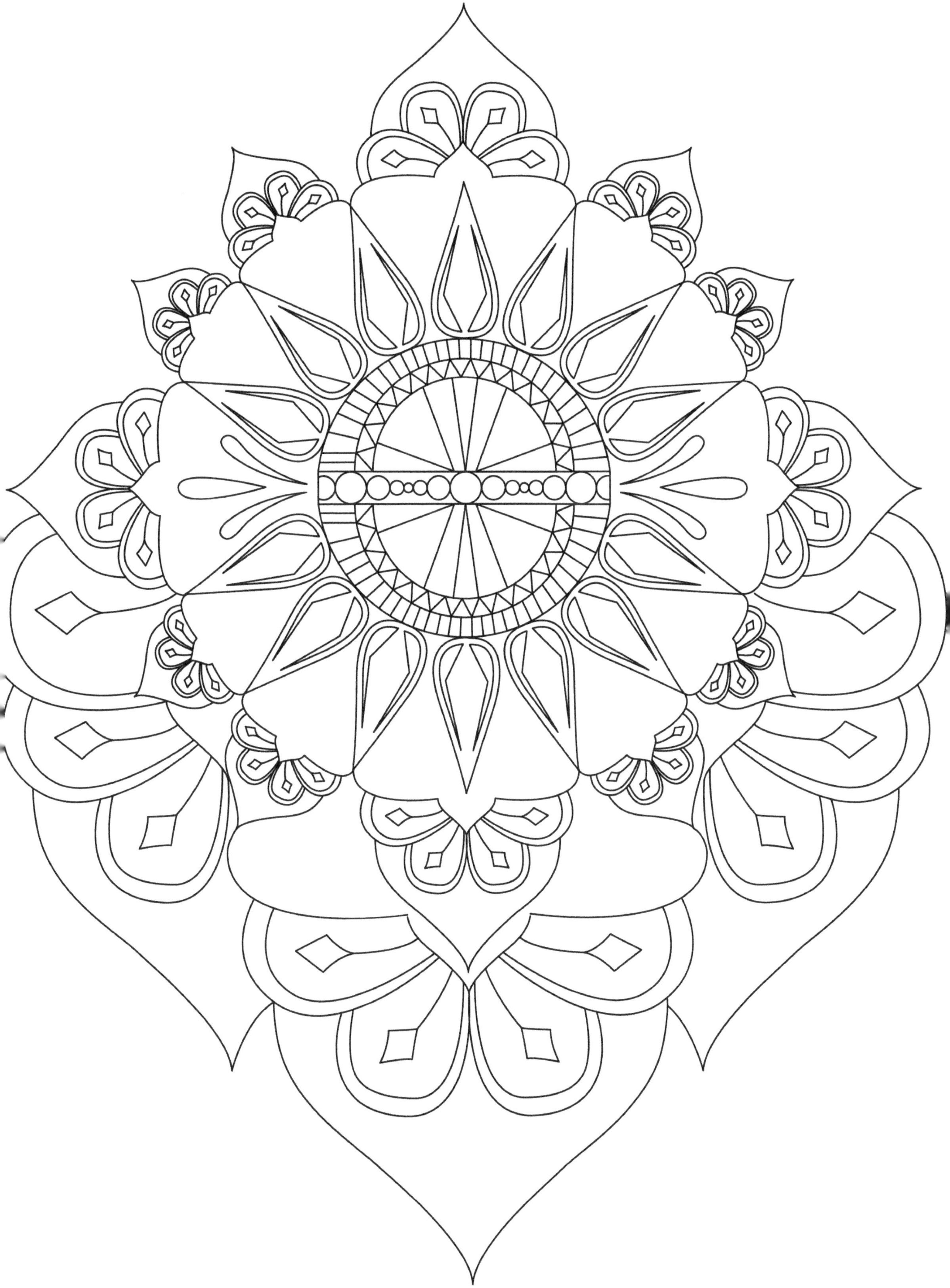

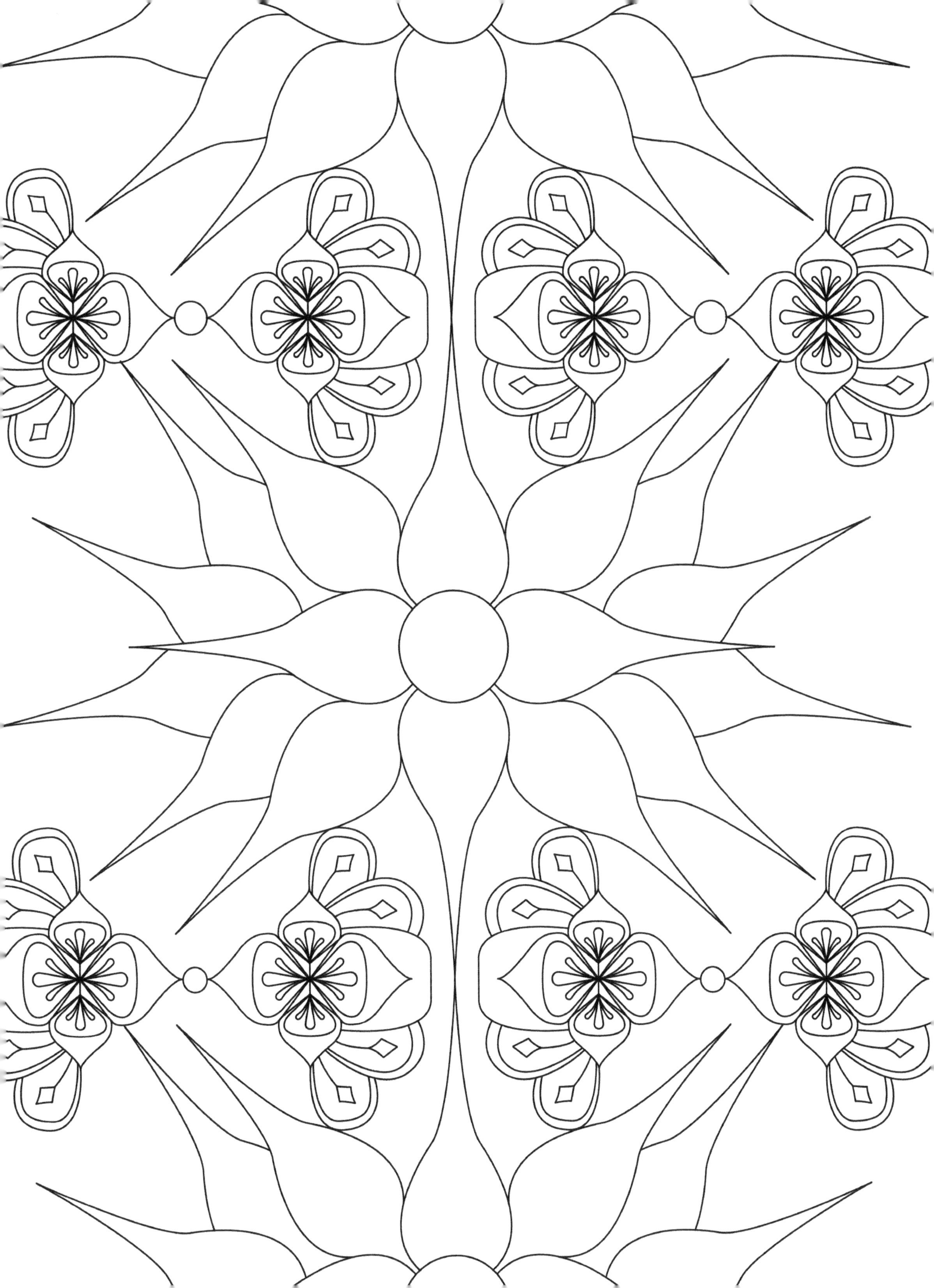

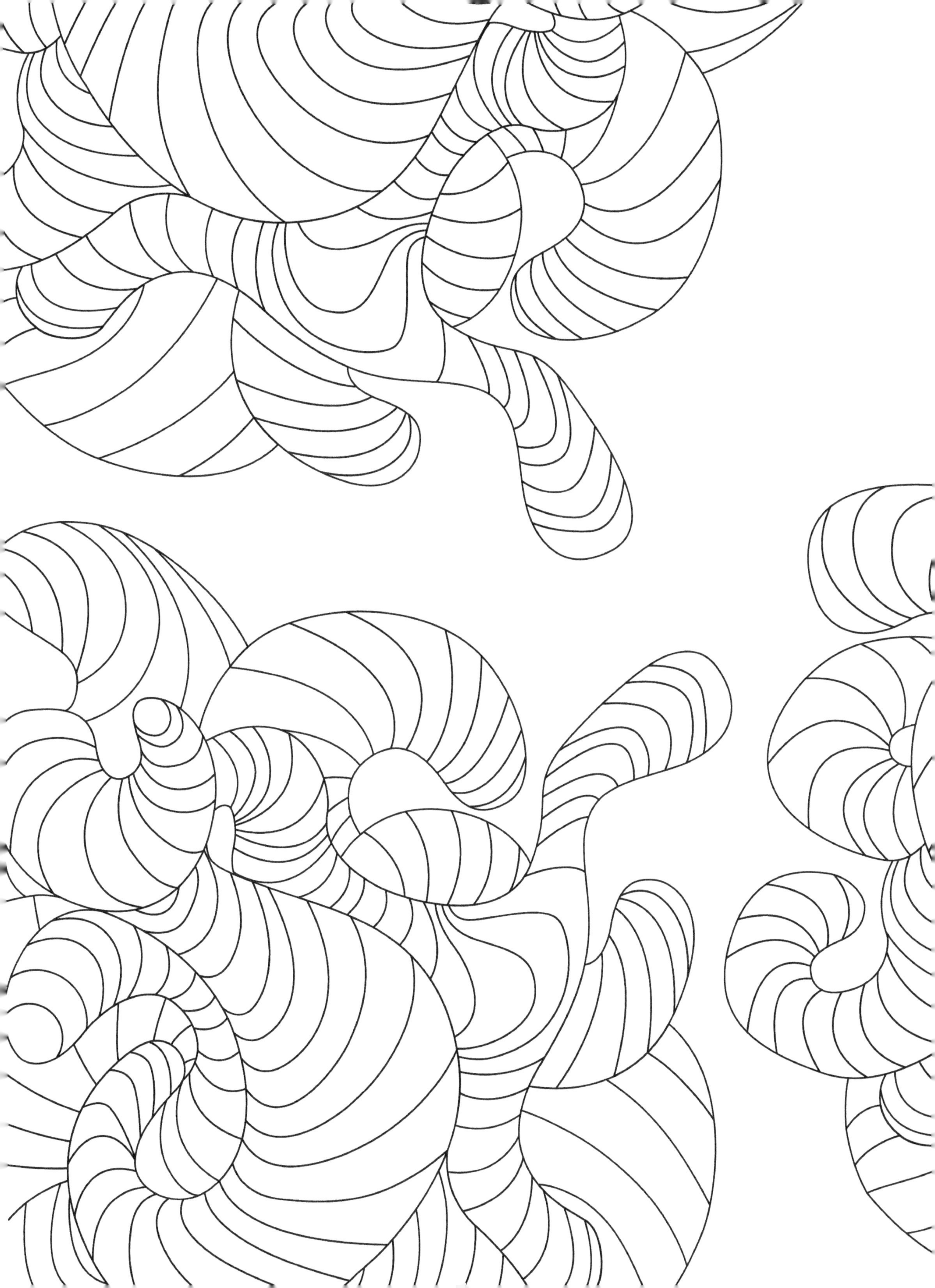

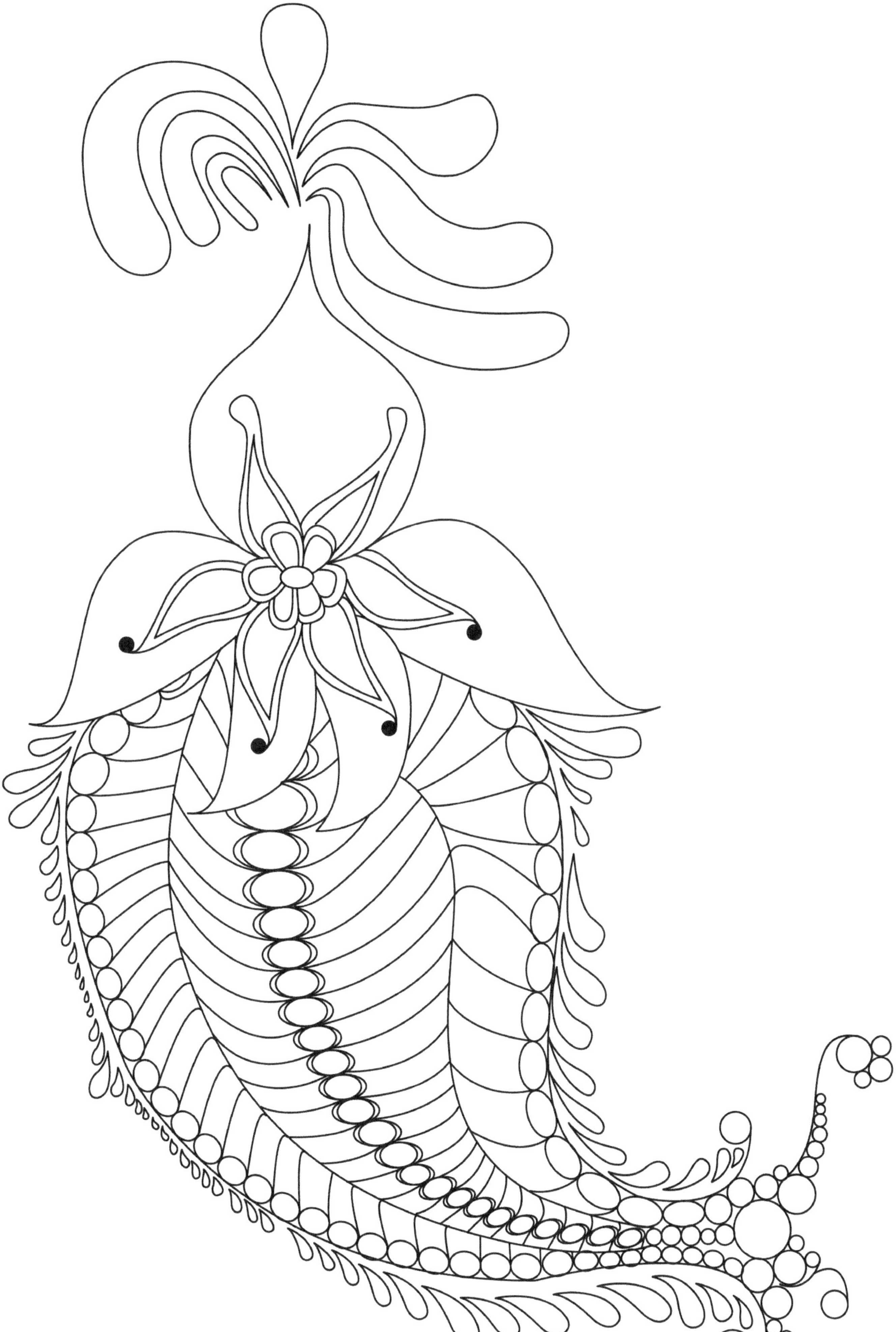

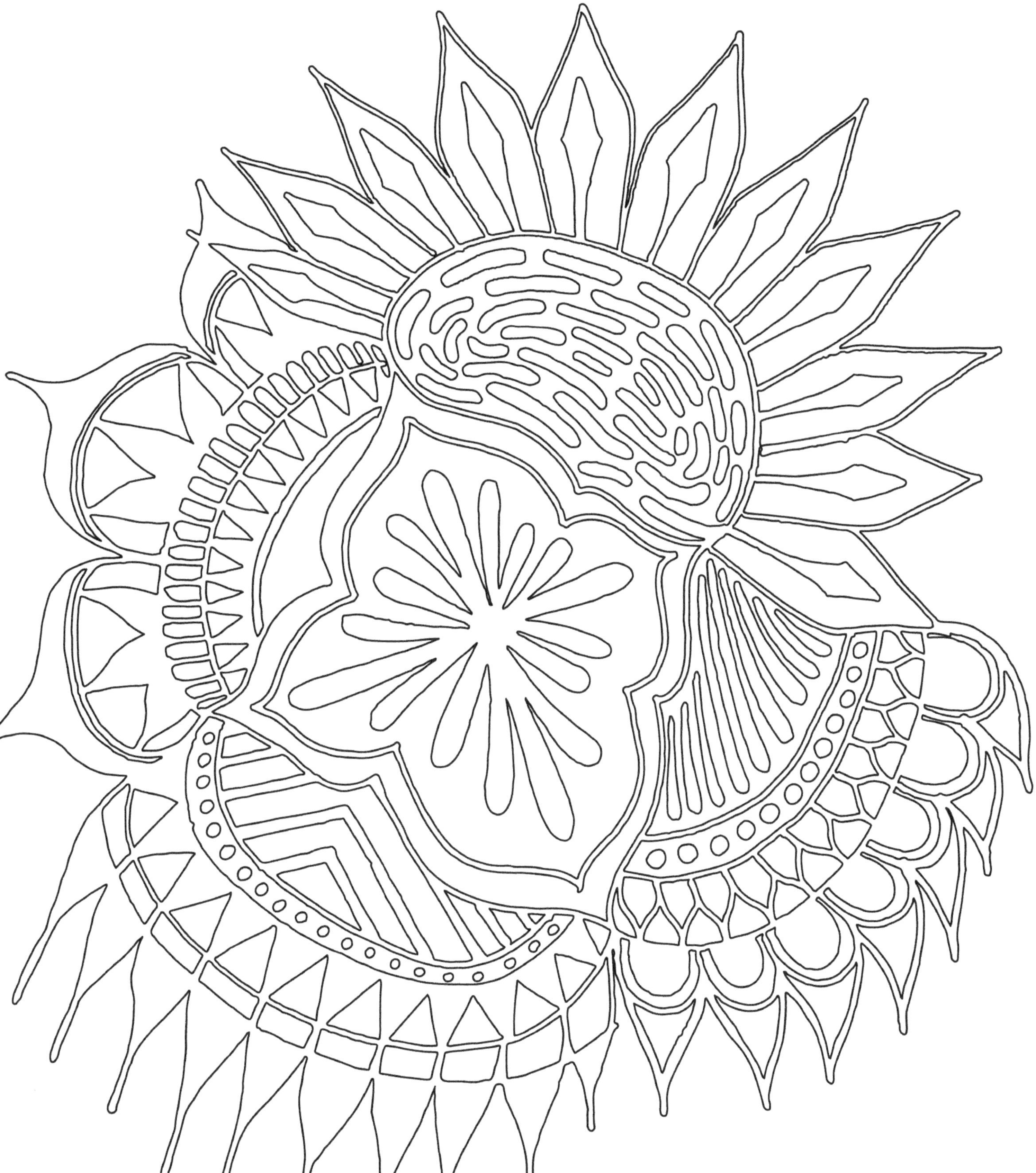

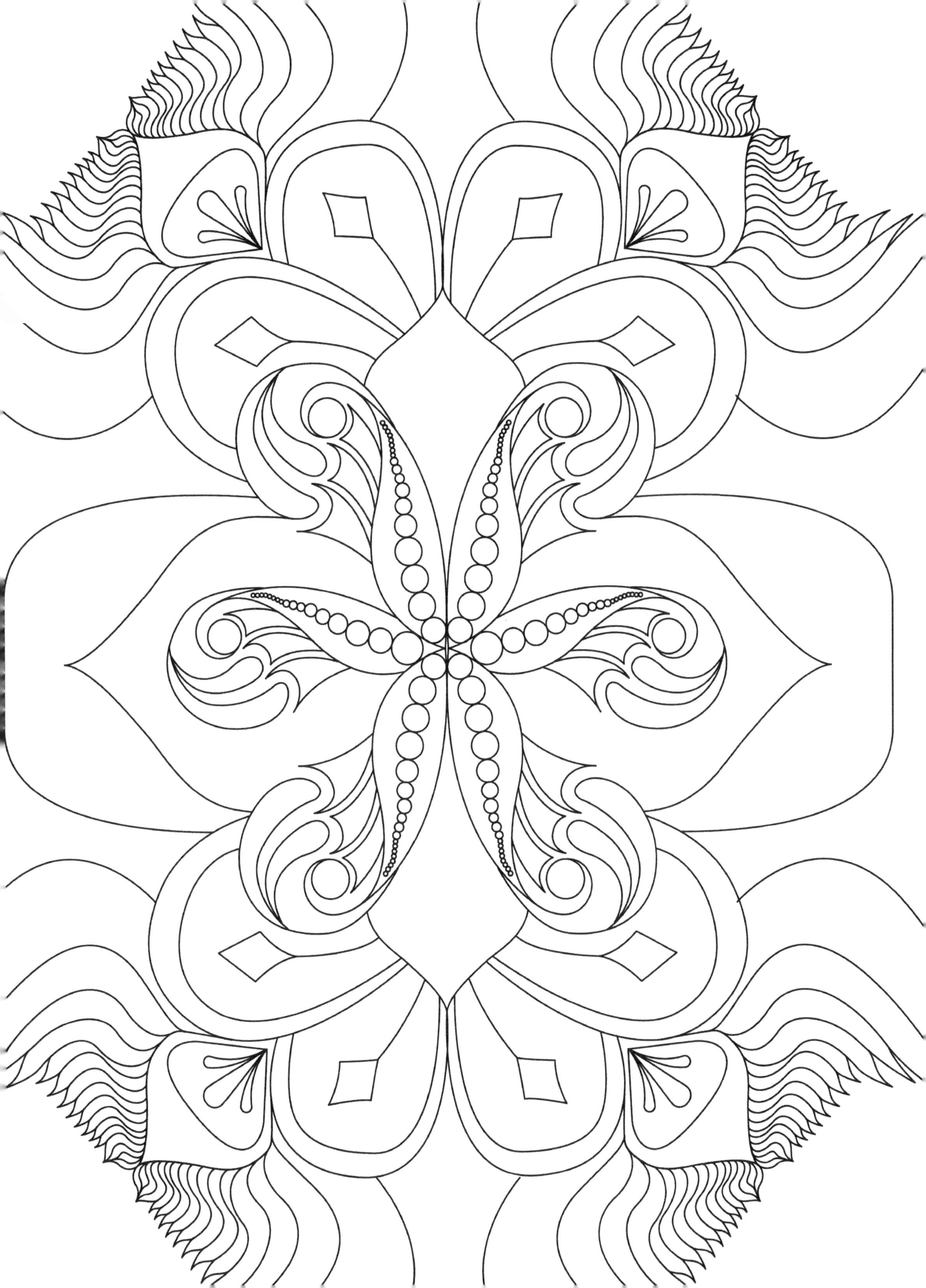

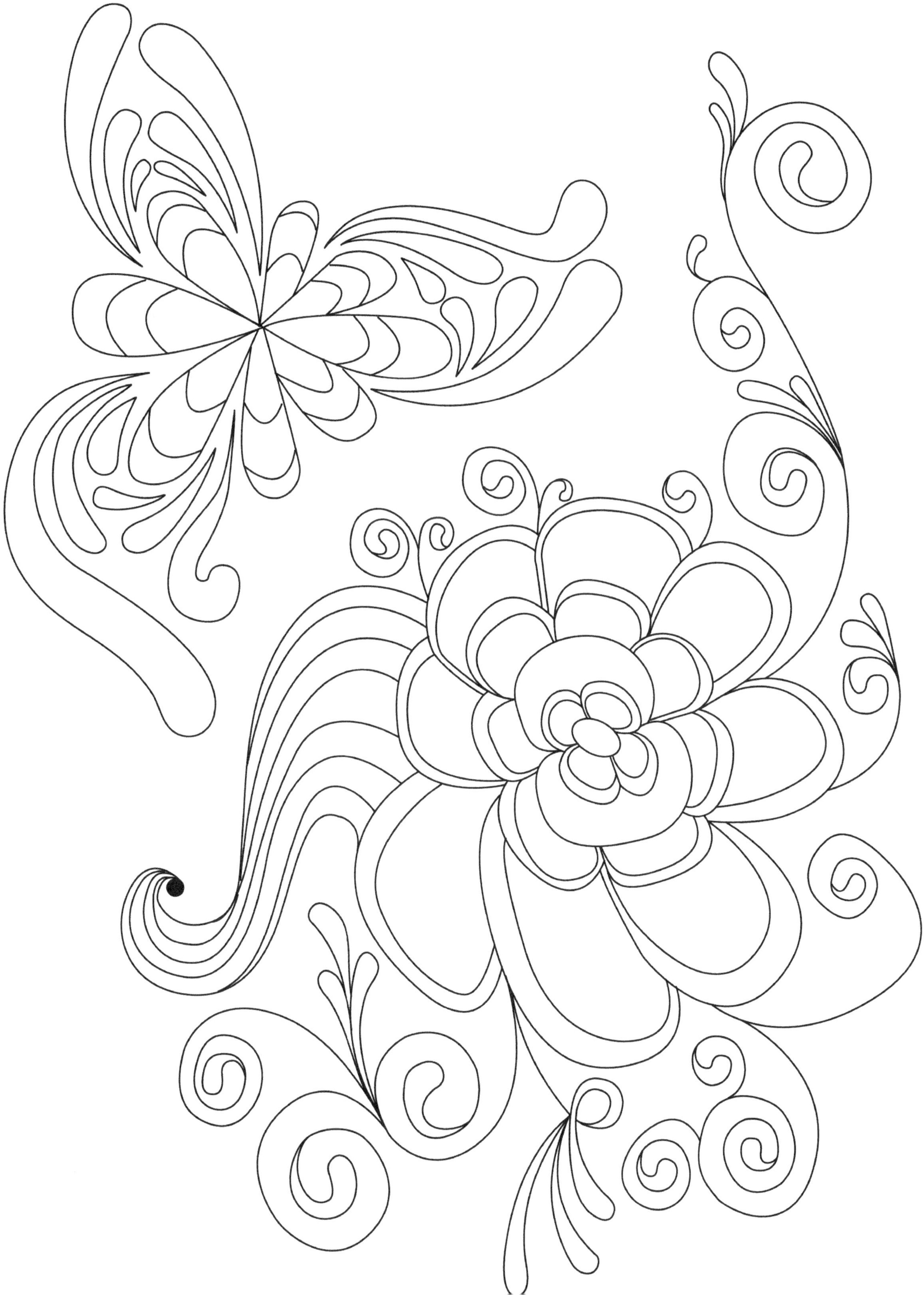

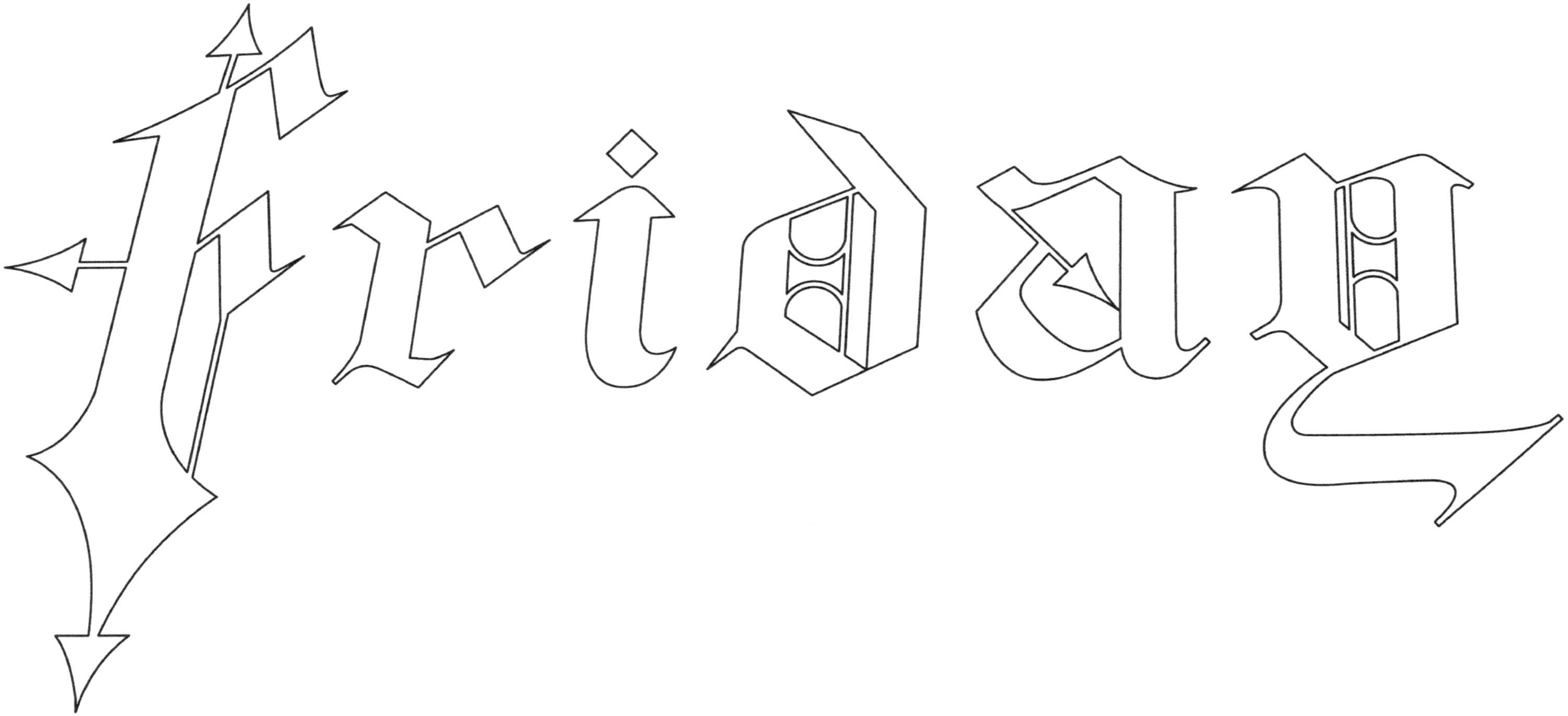
Friday

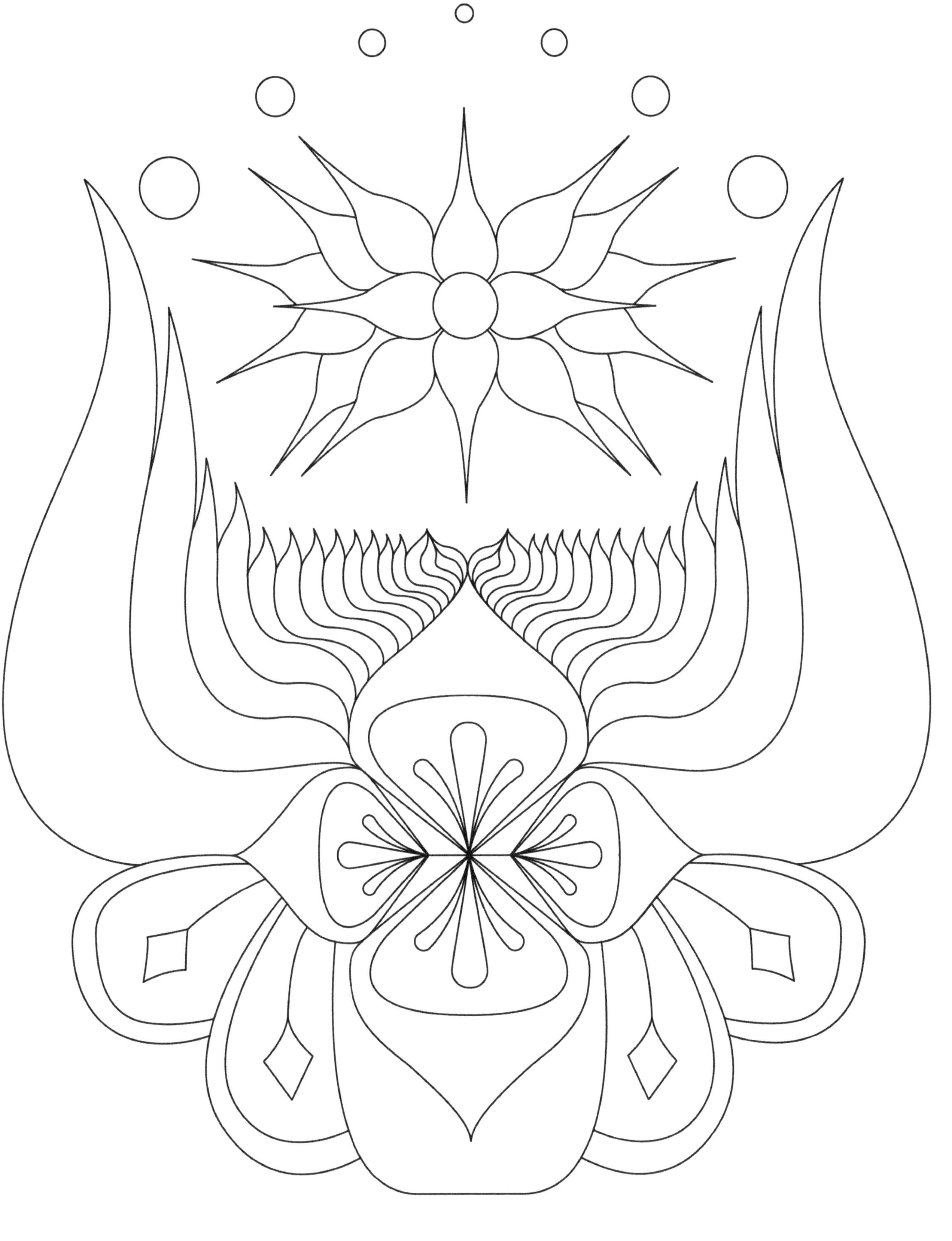

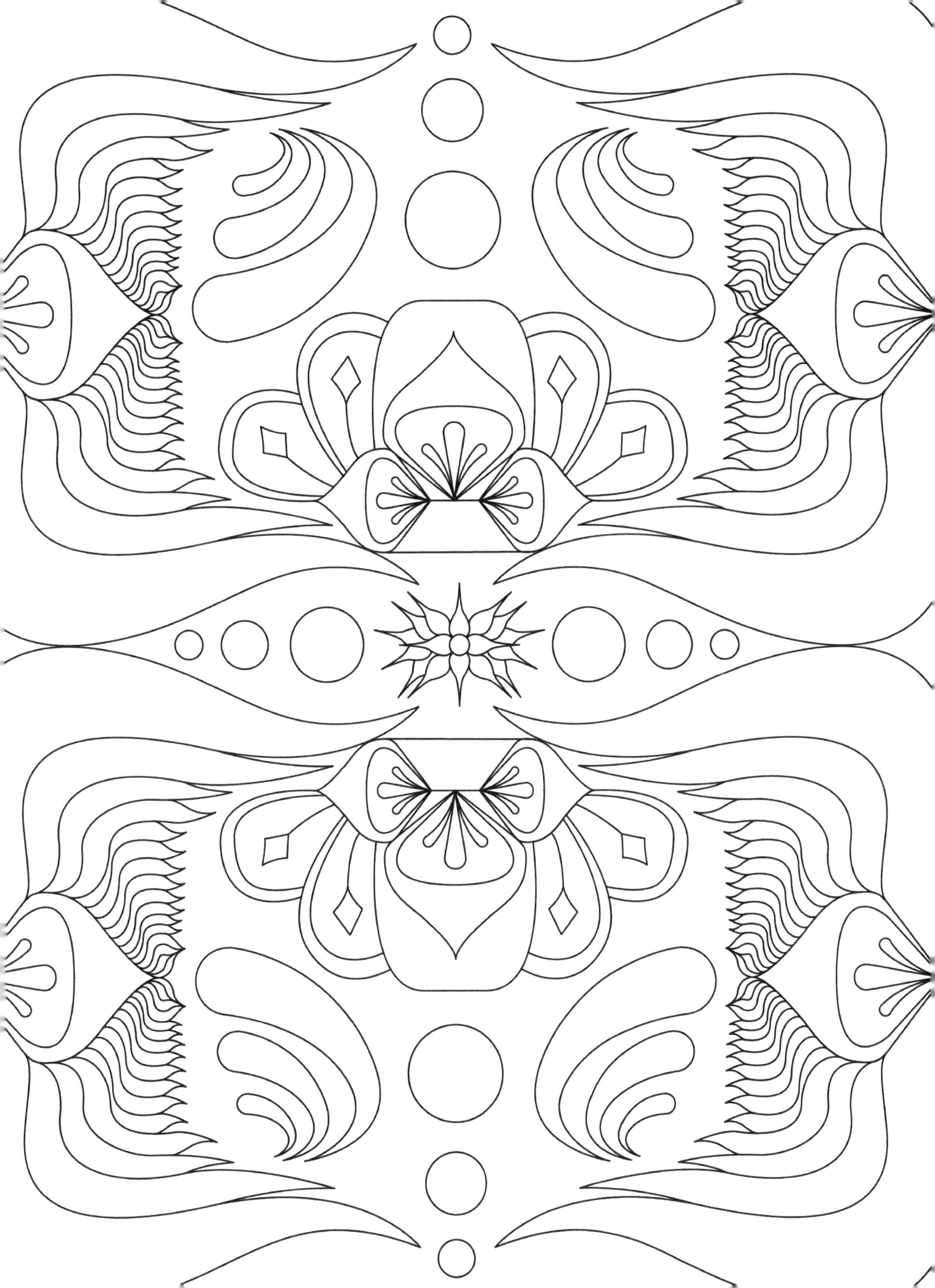

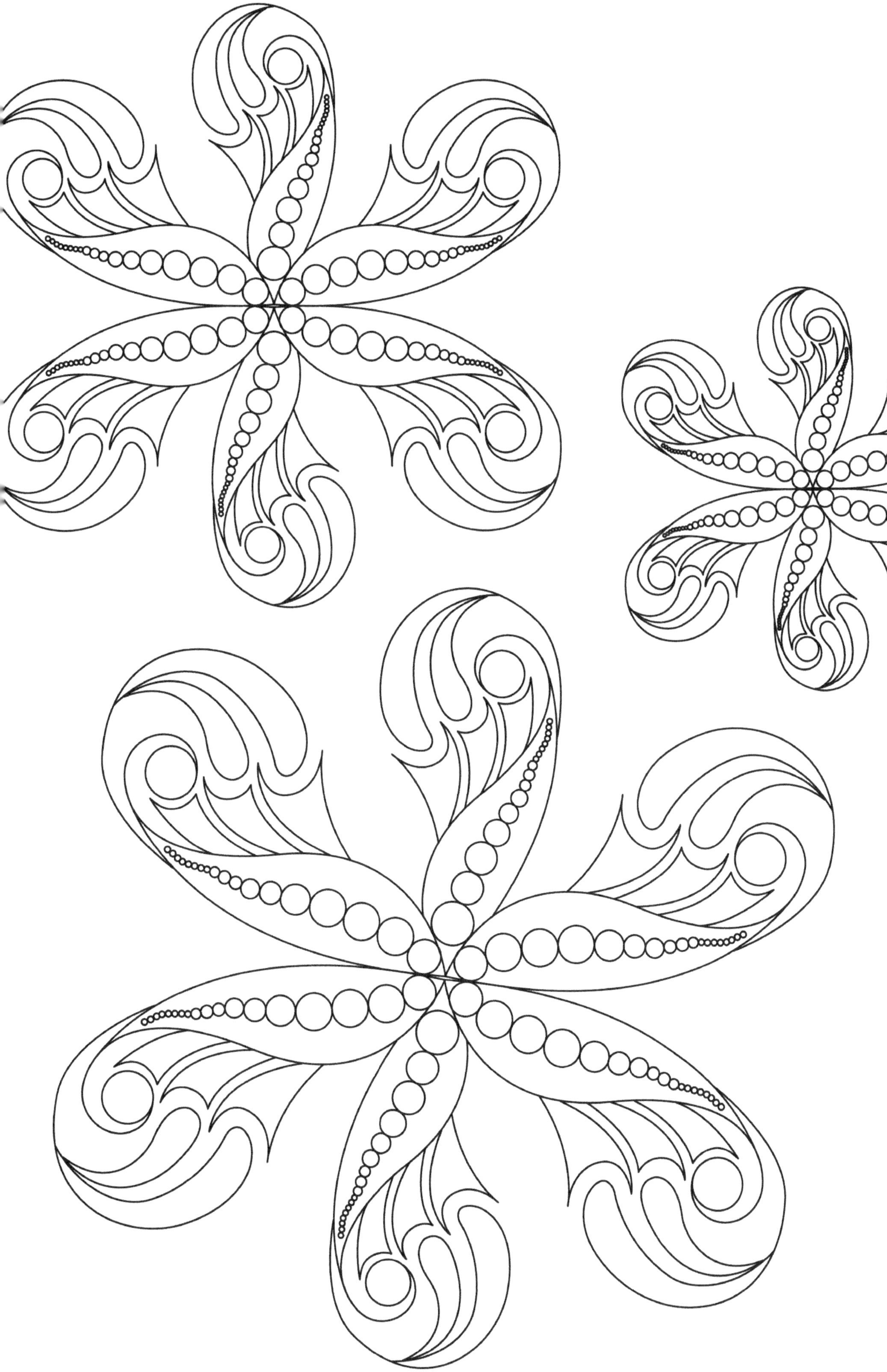

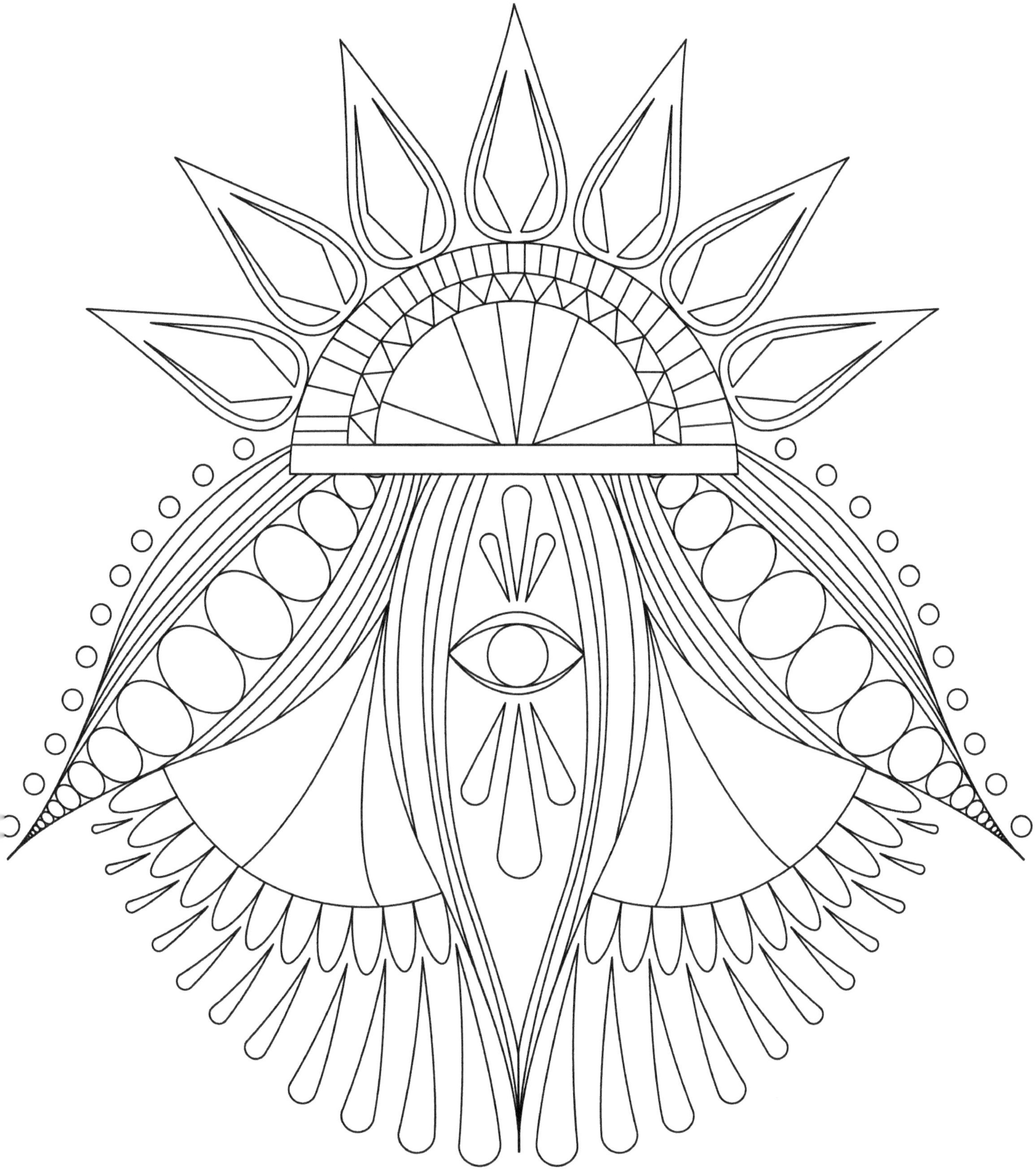

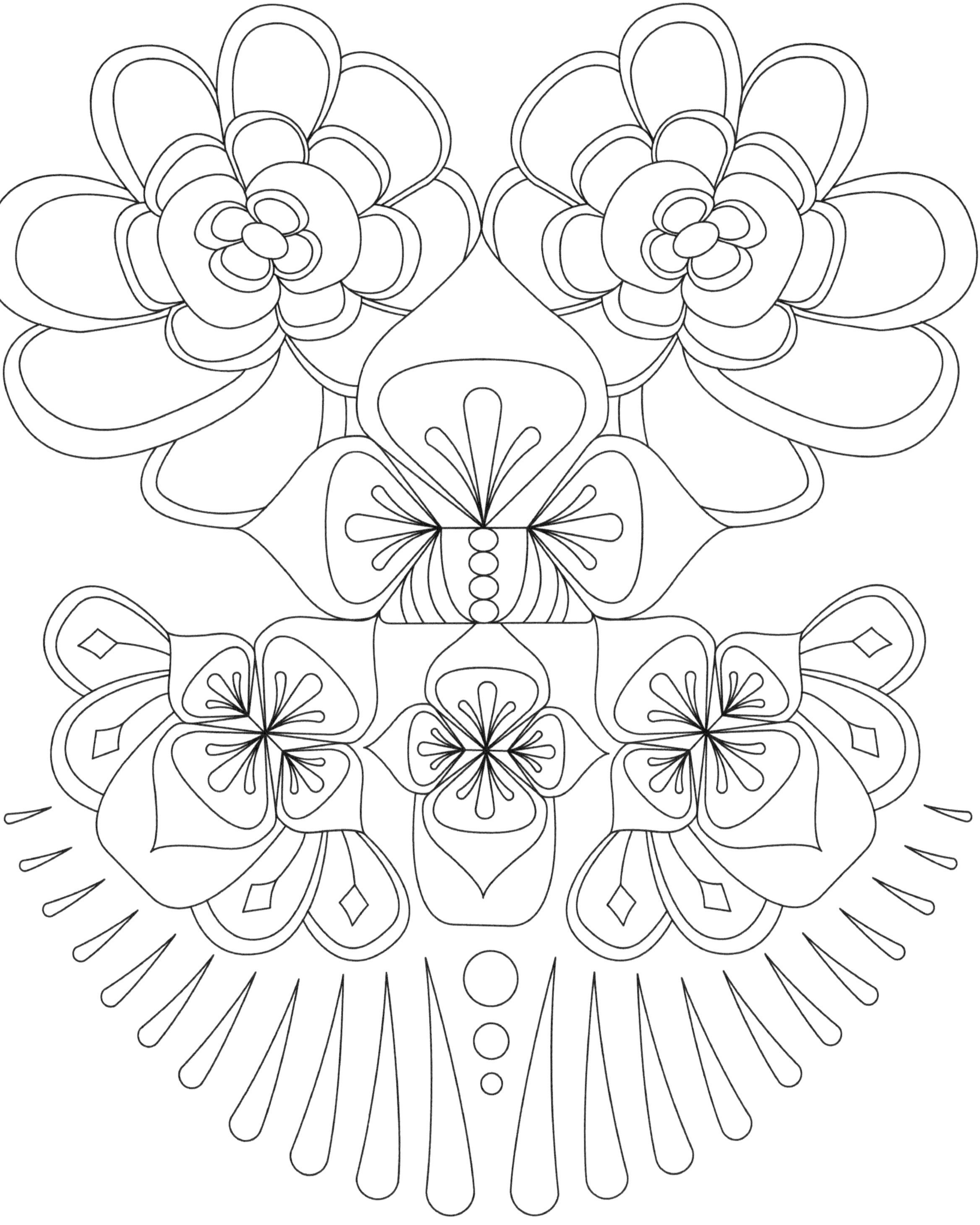

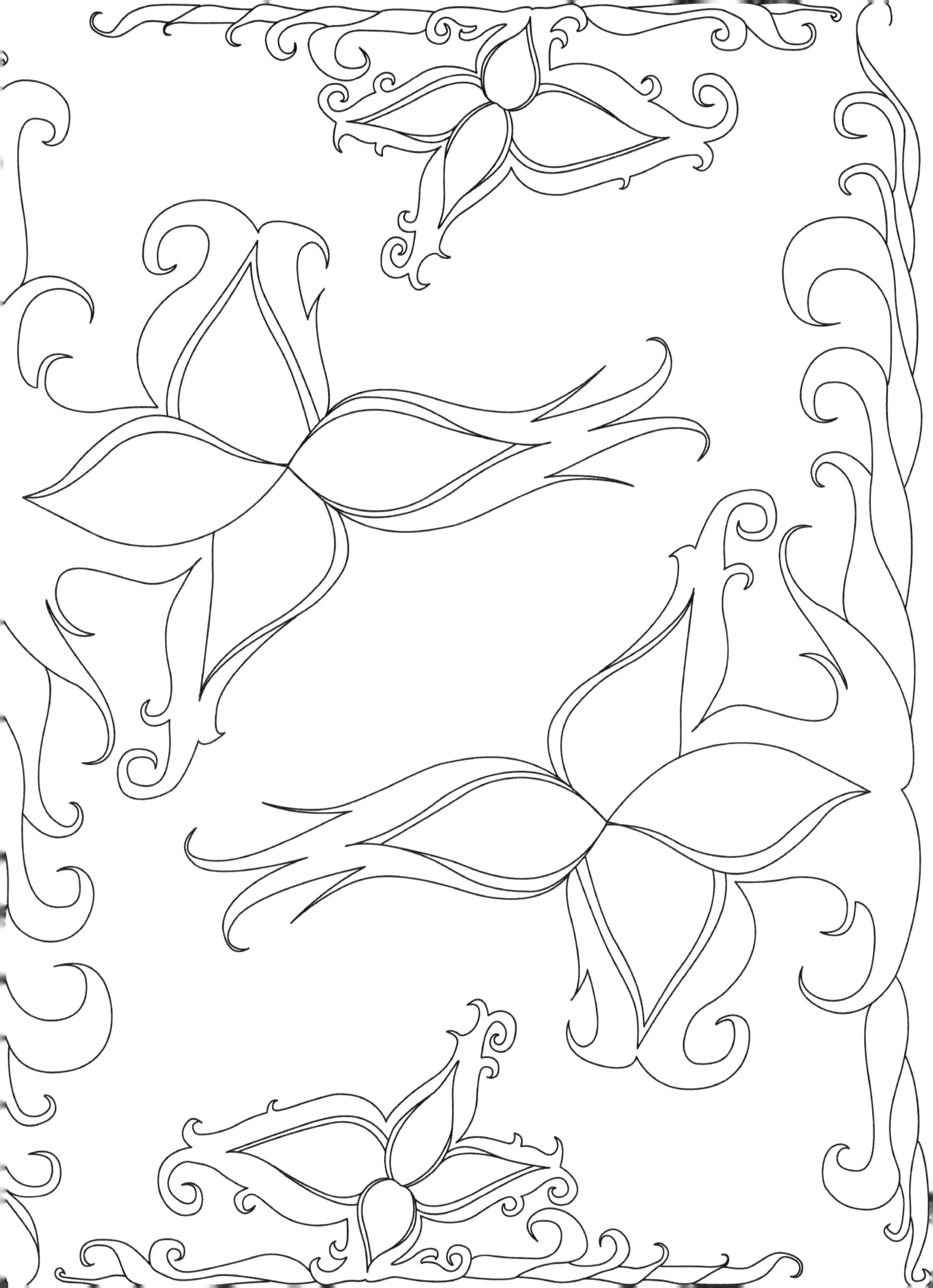

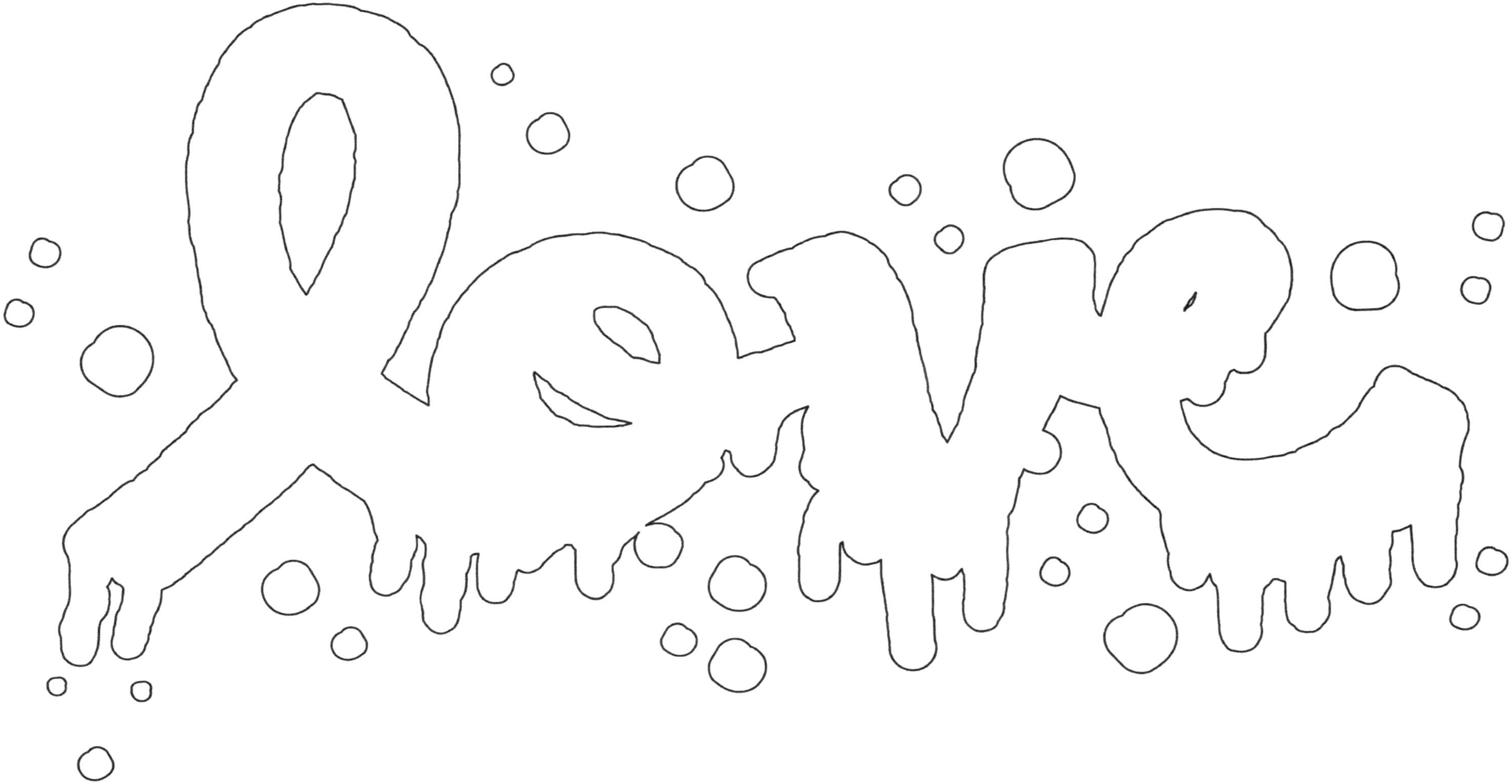
love

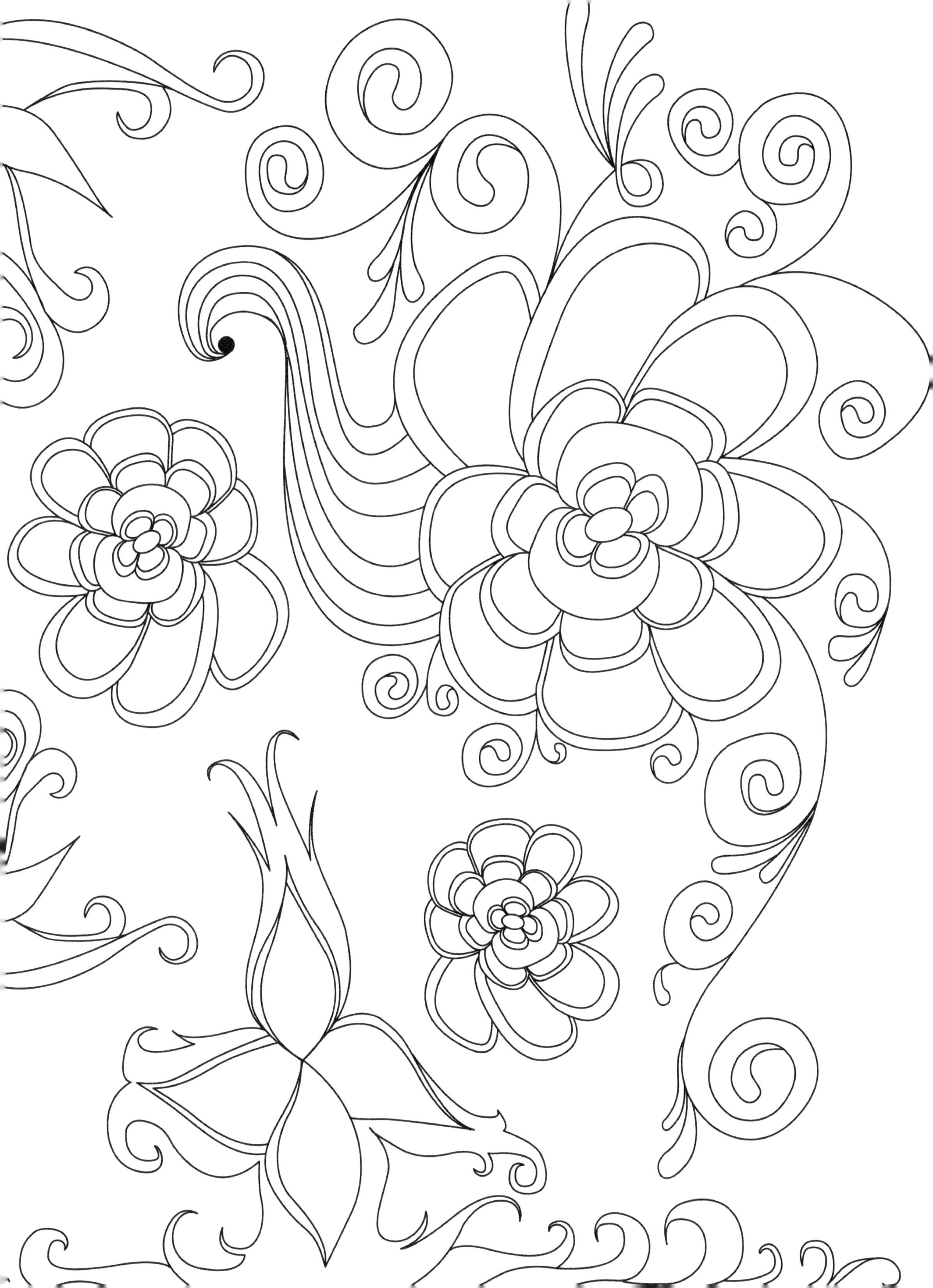

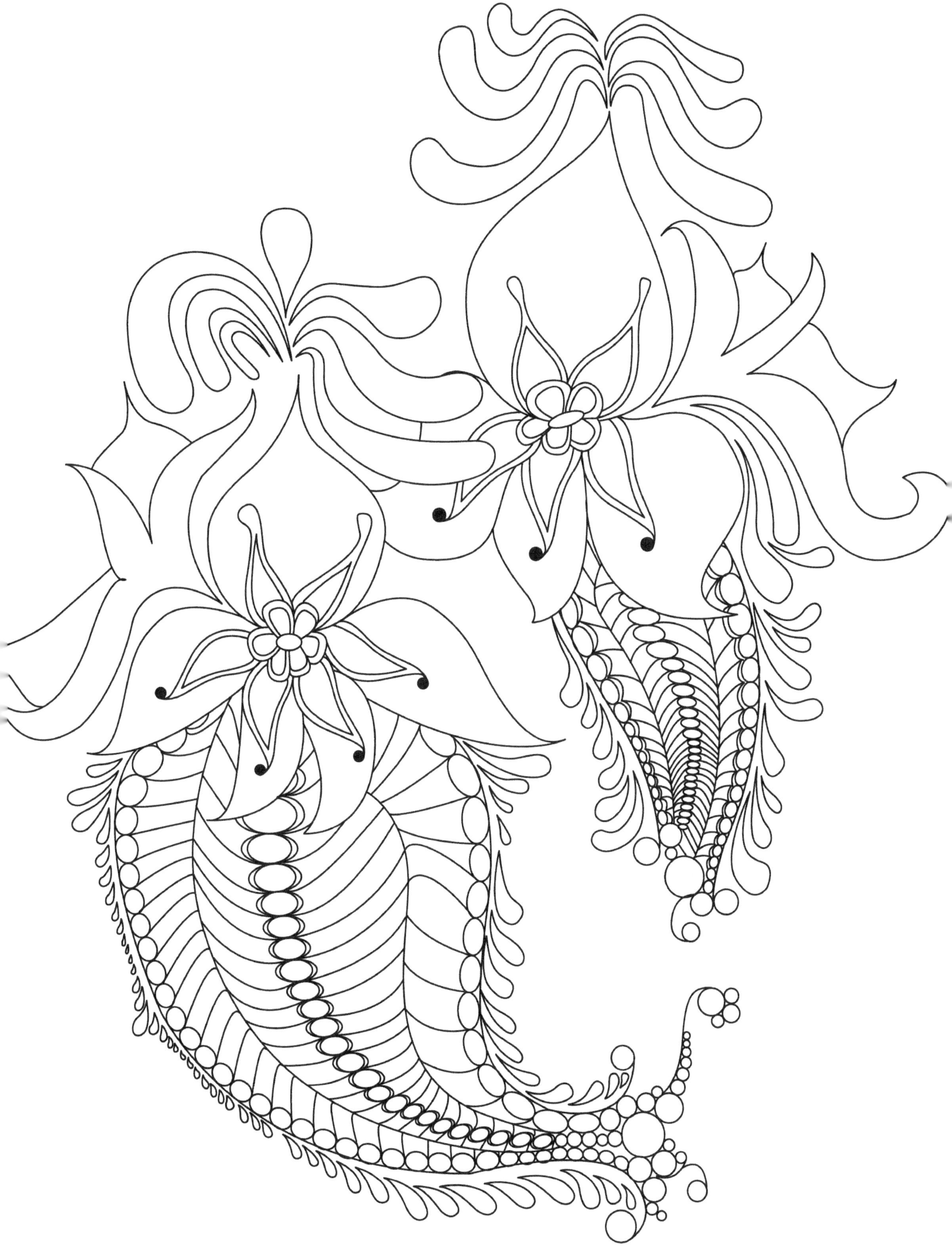

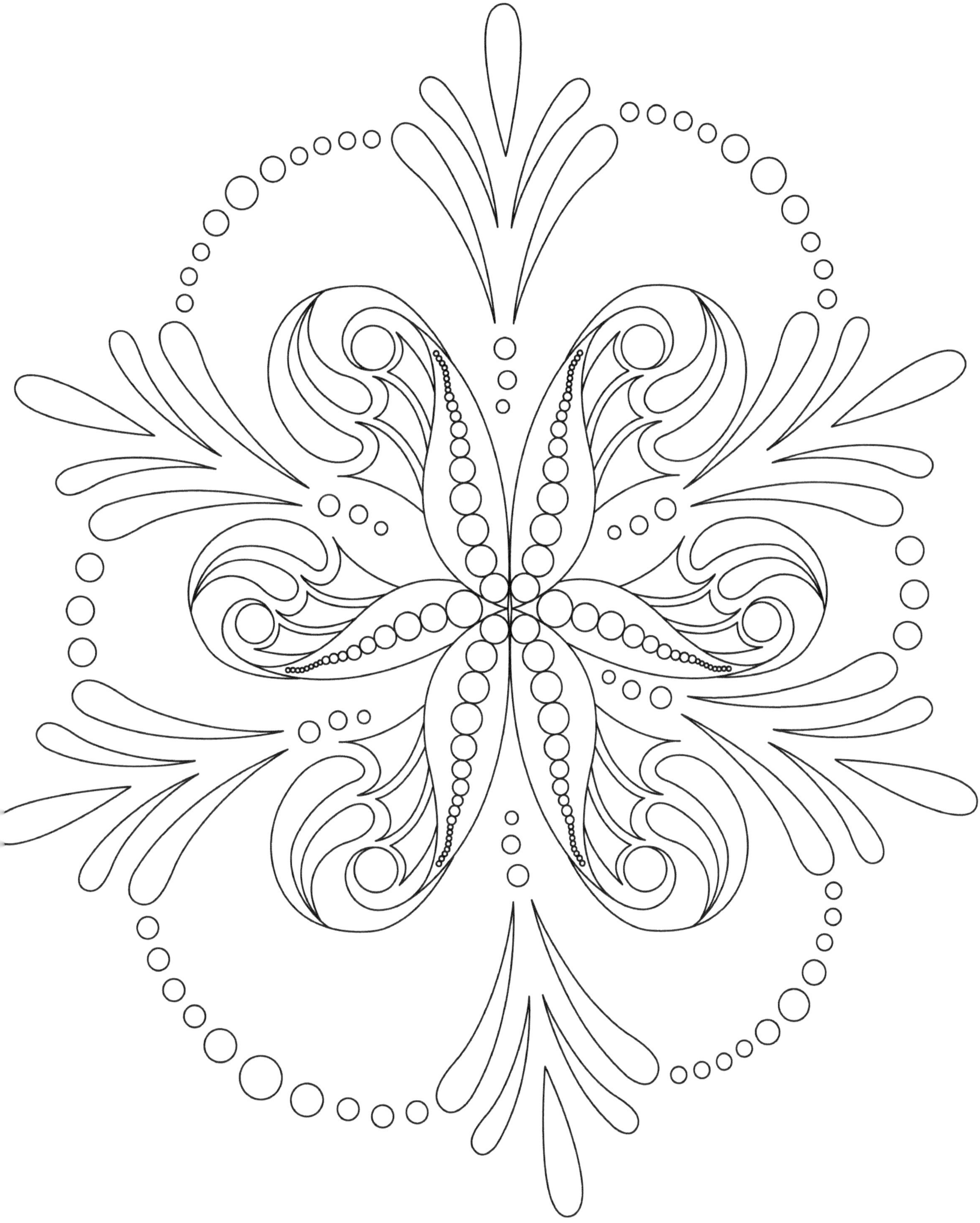

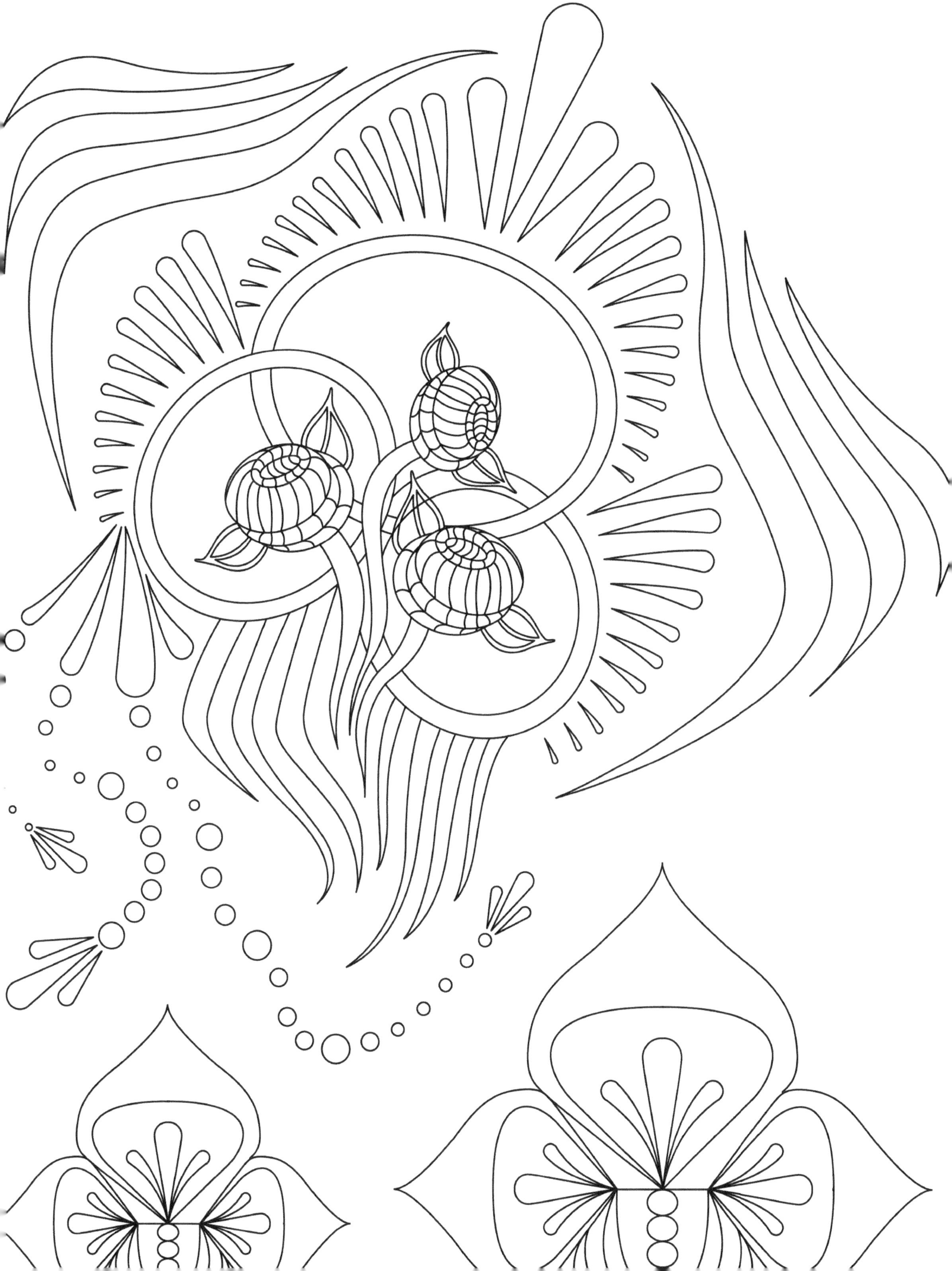

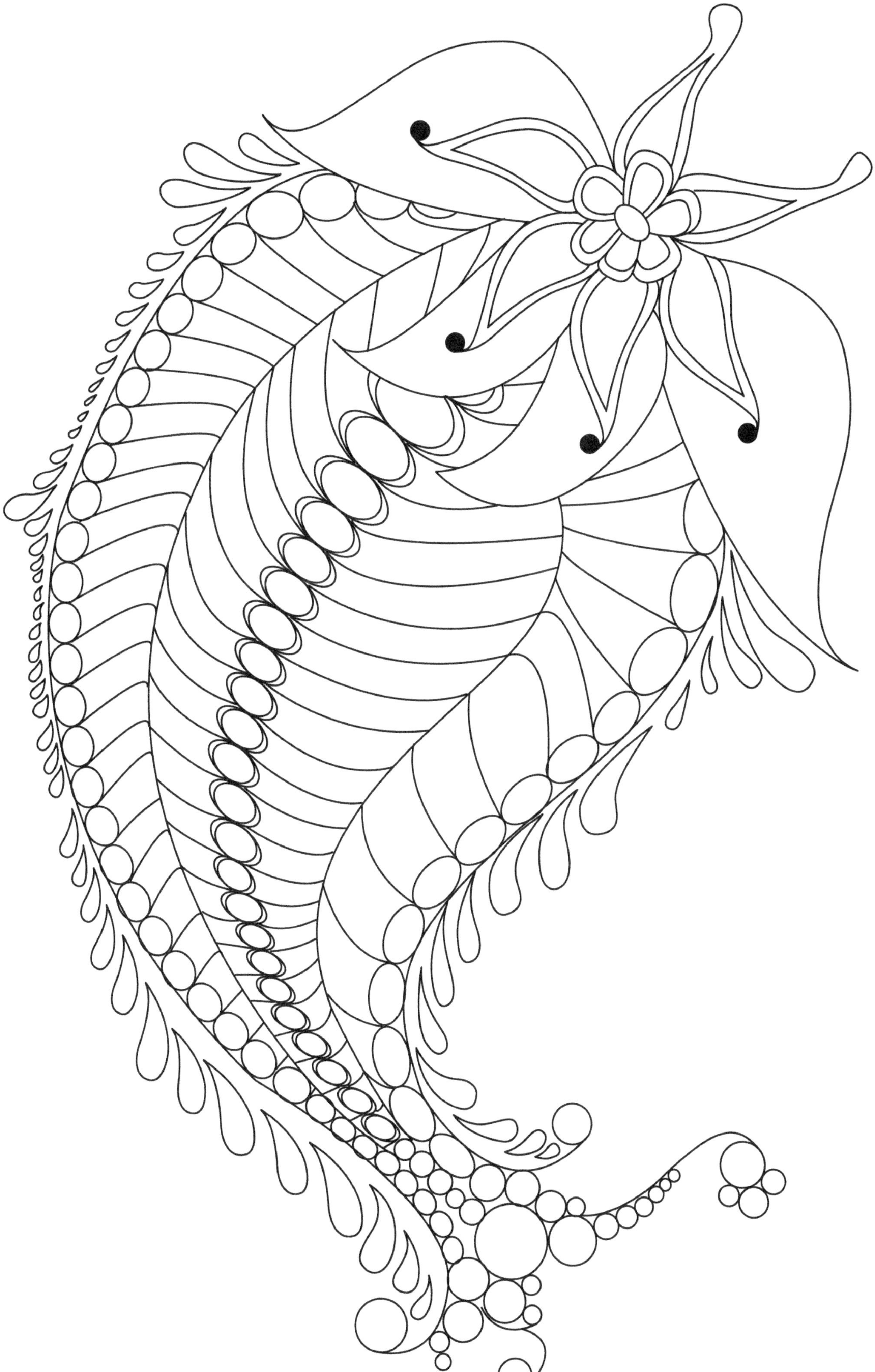

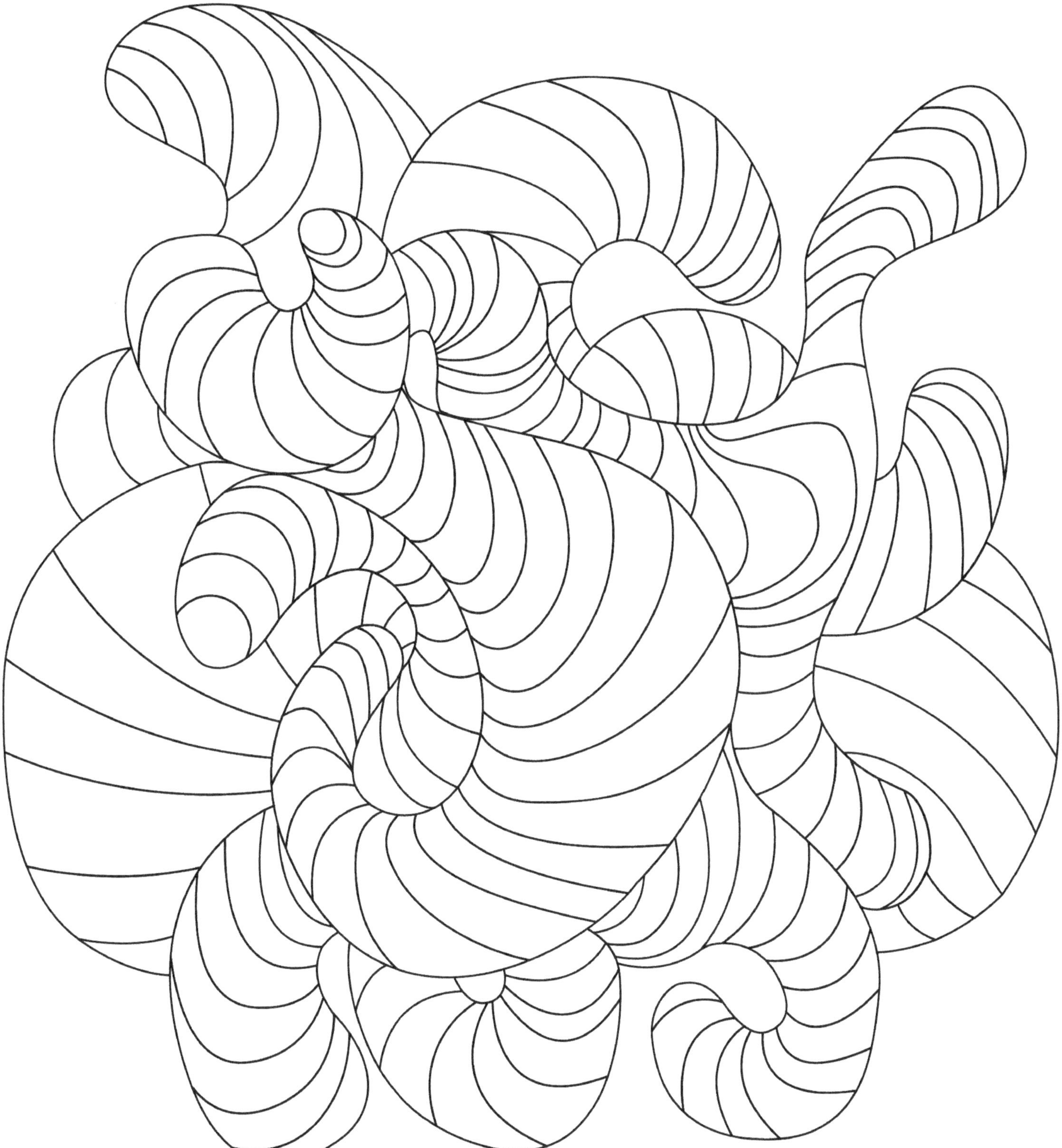

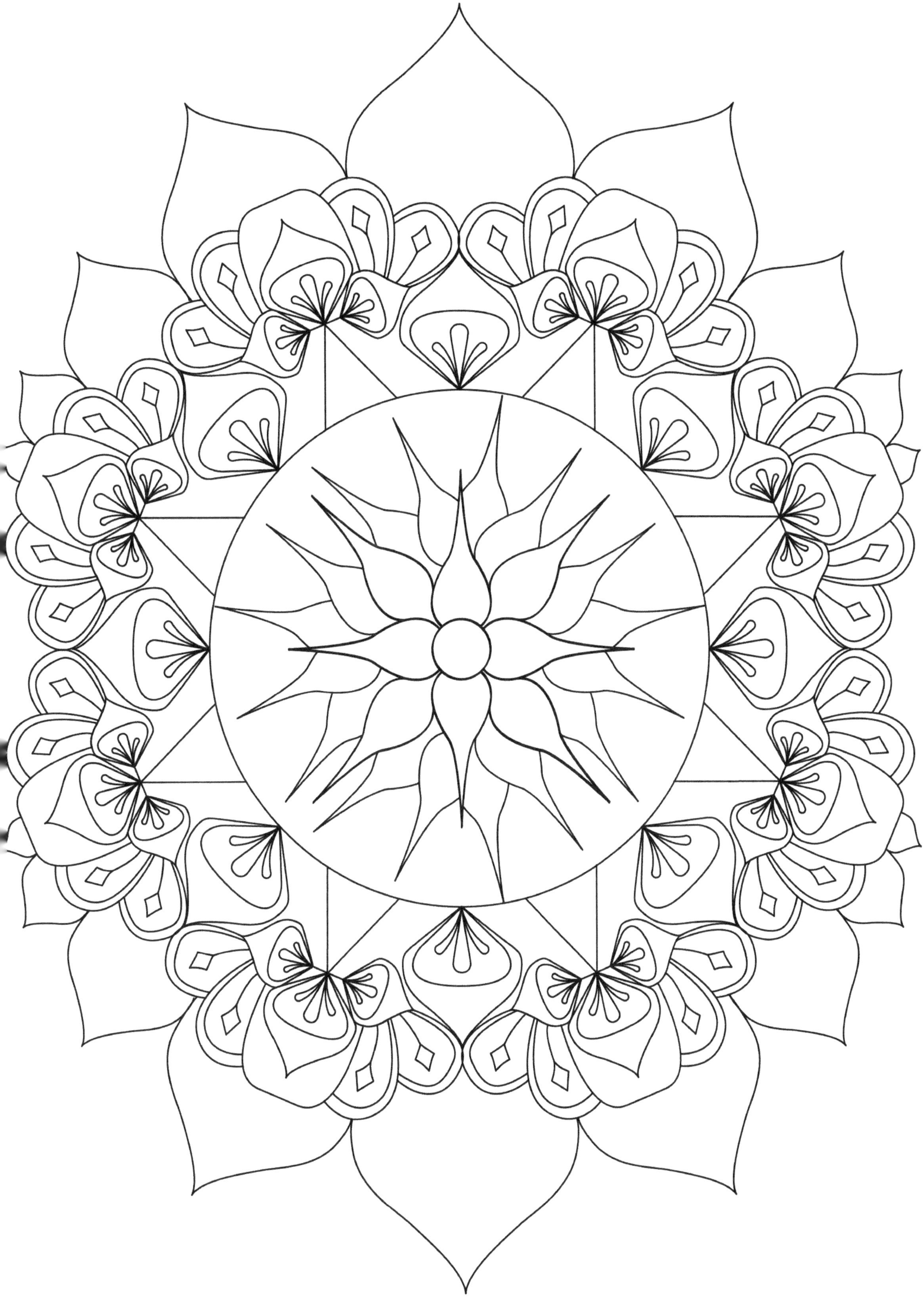

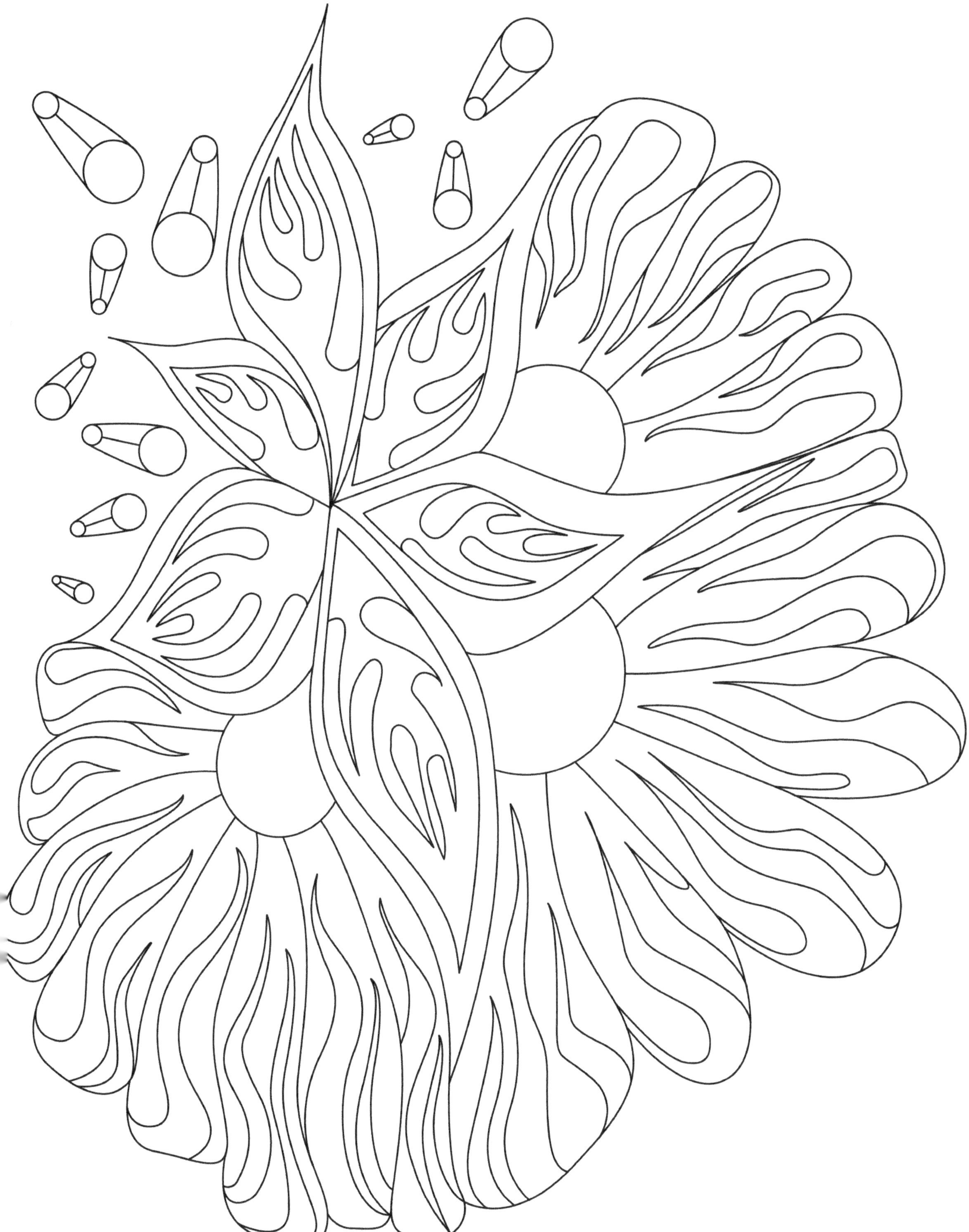

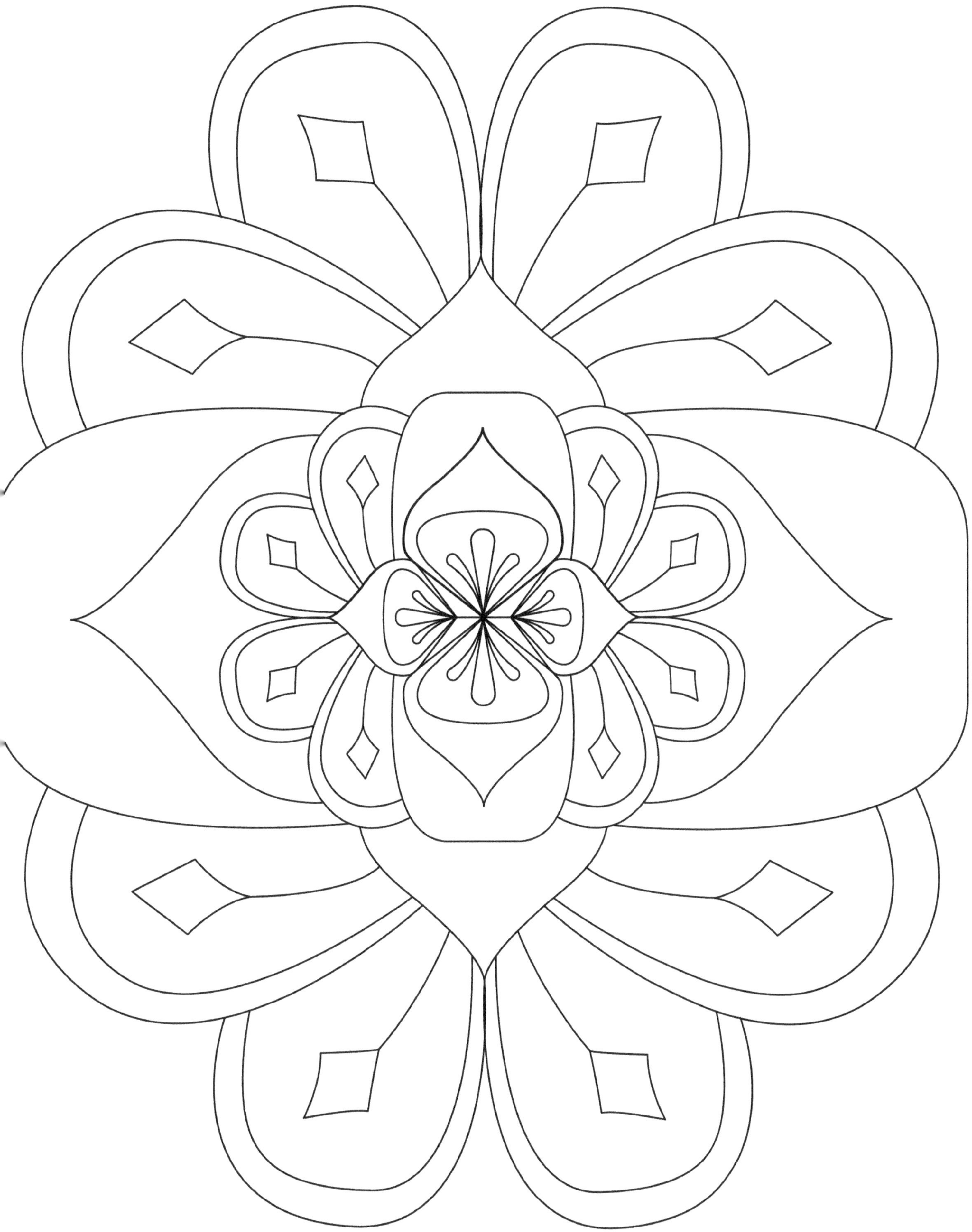

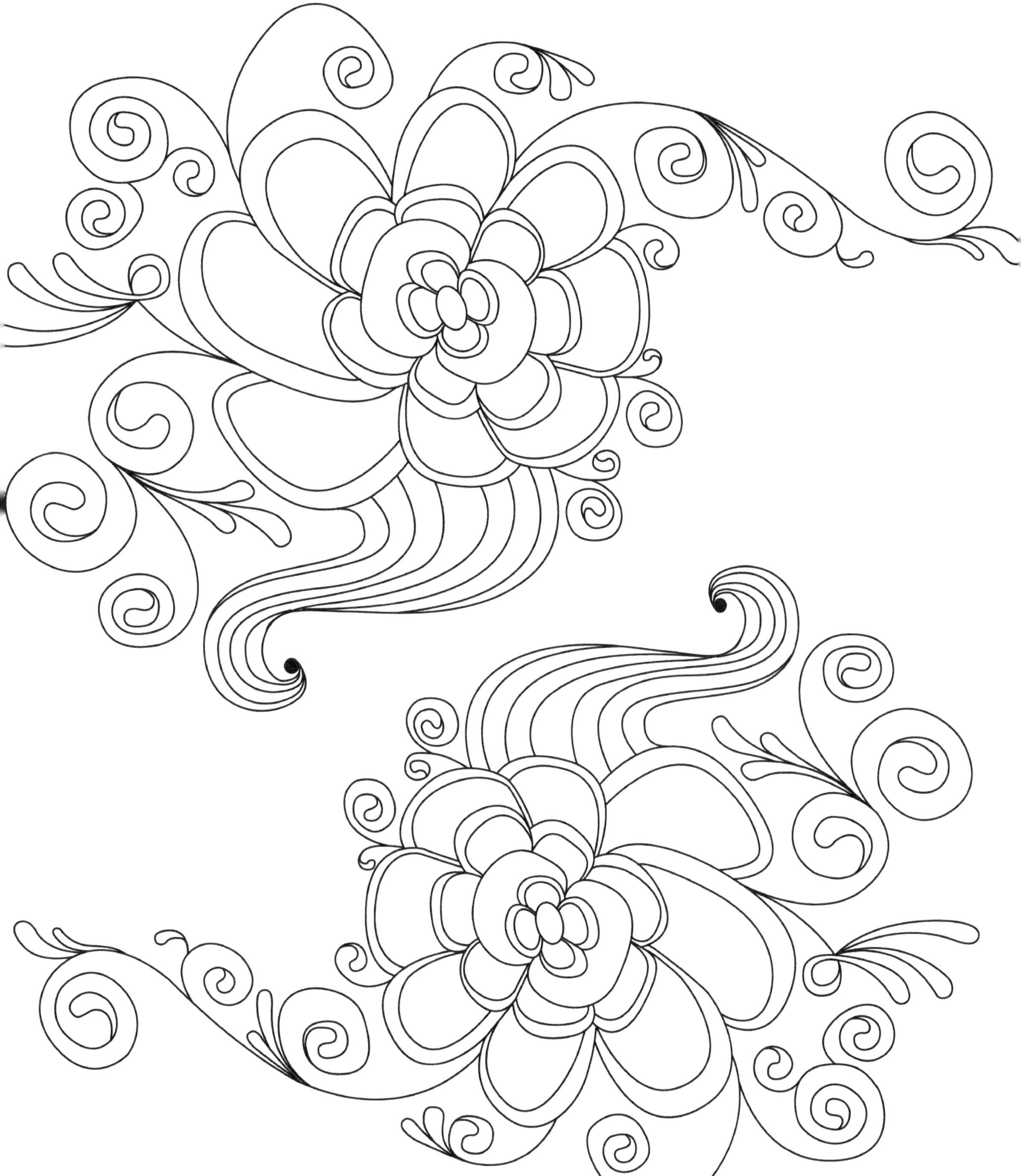

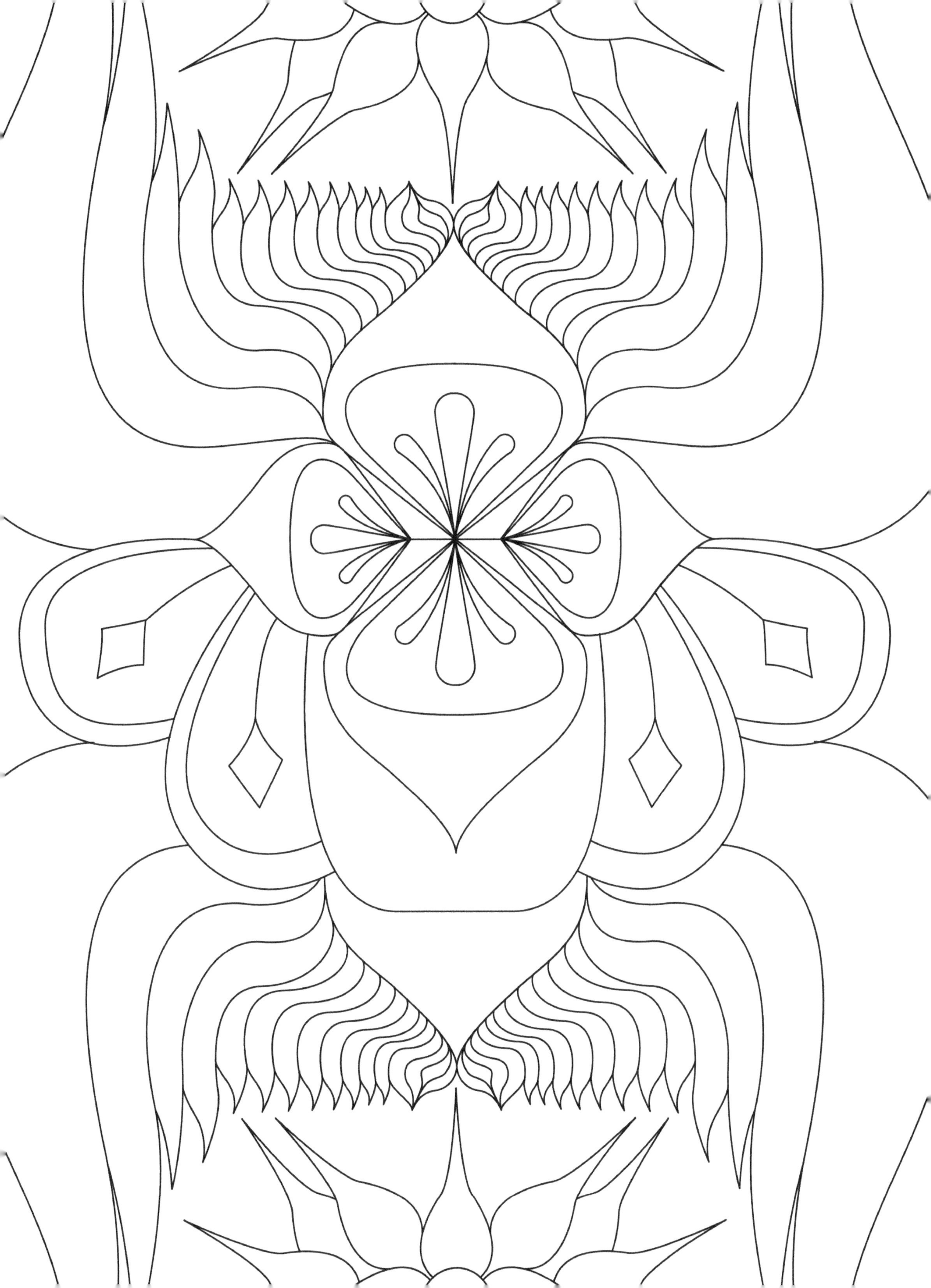

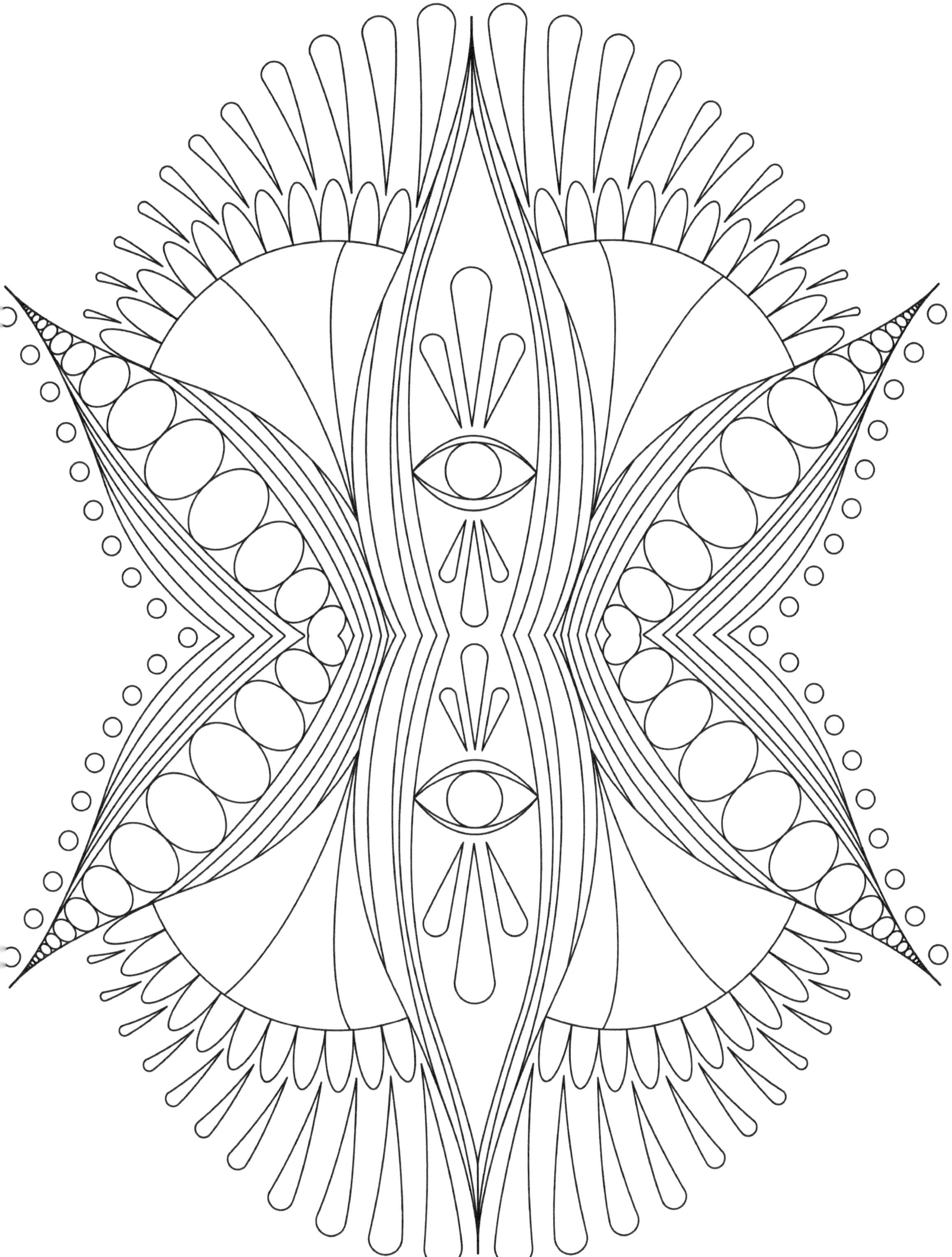

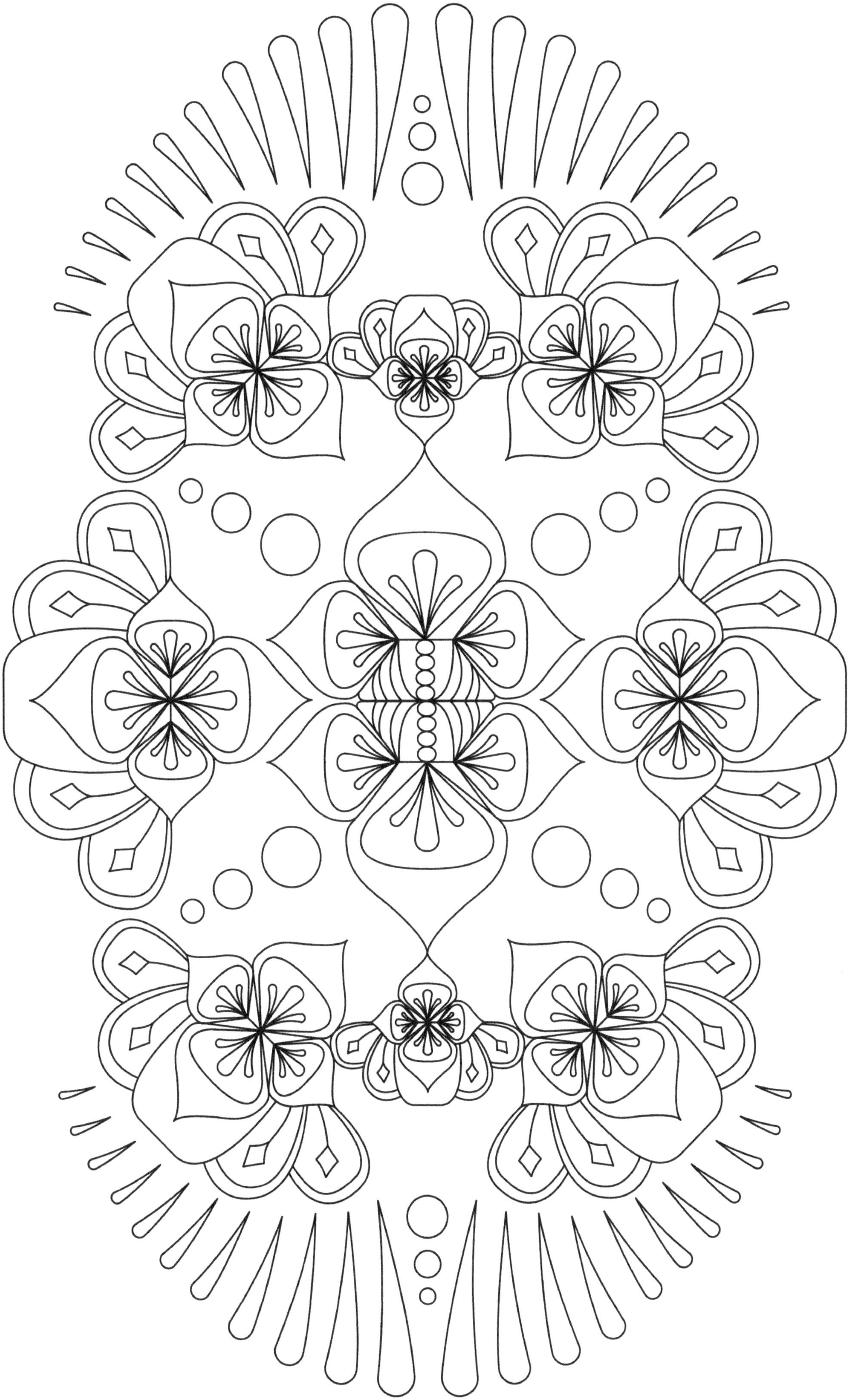

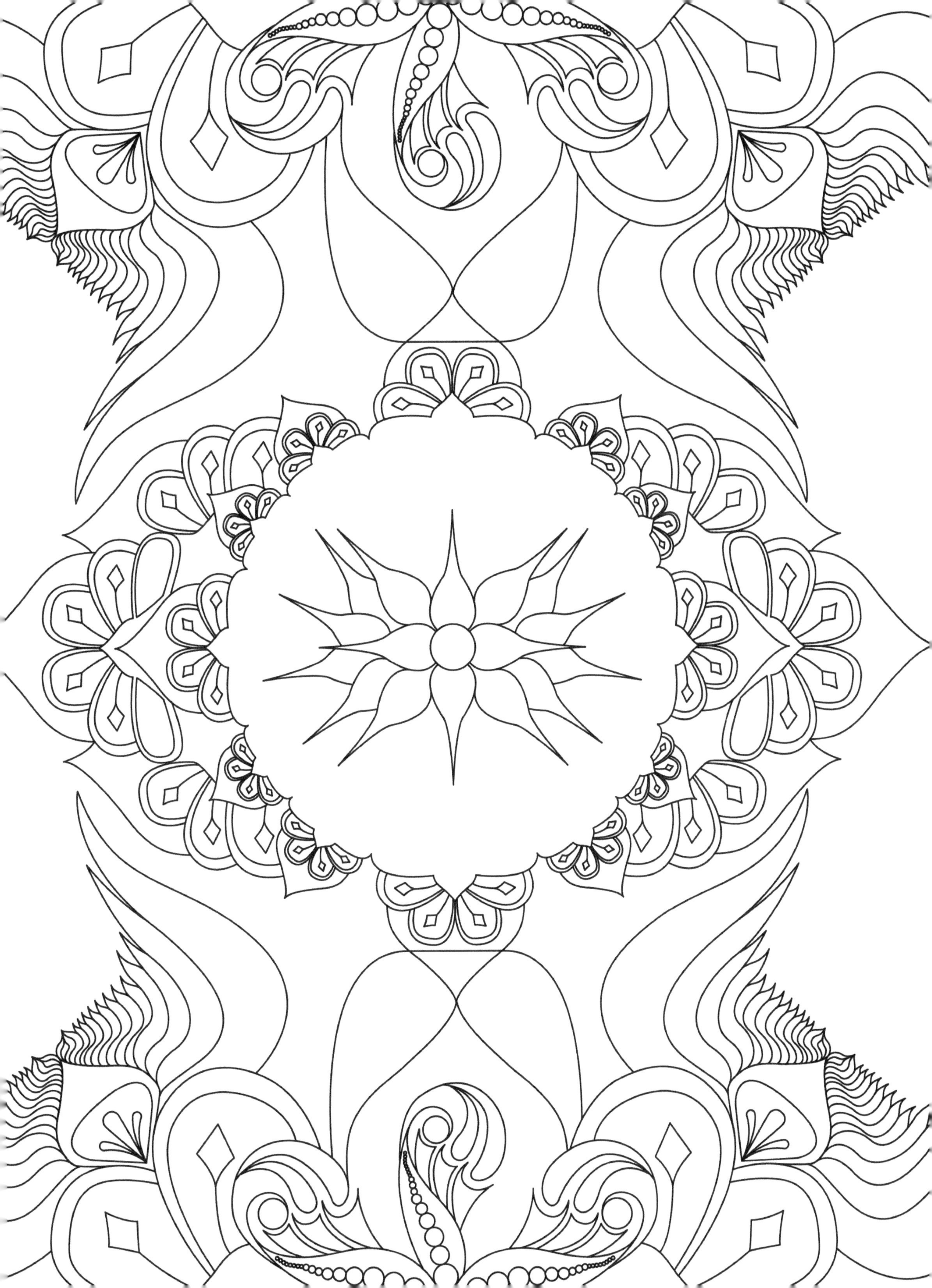

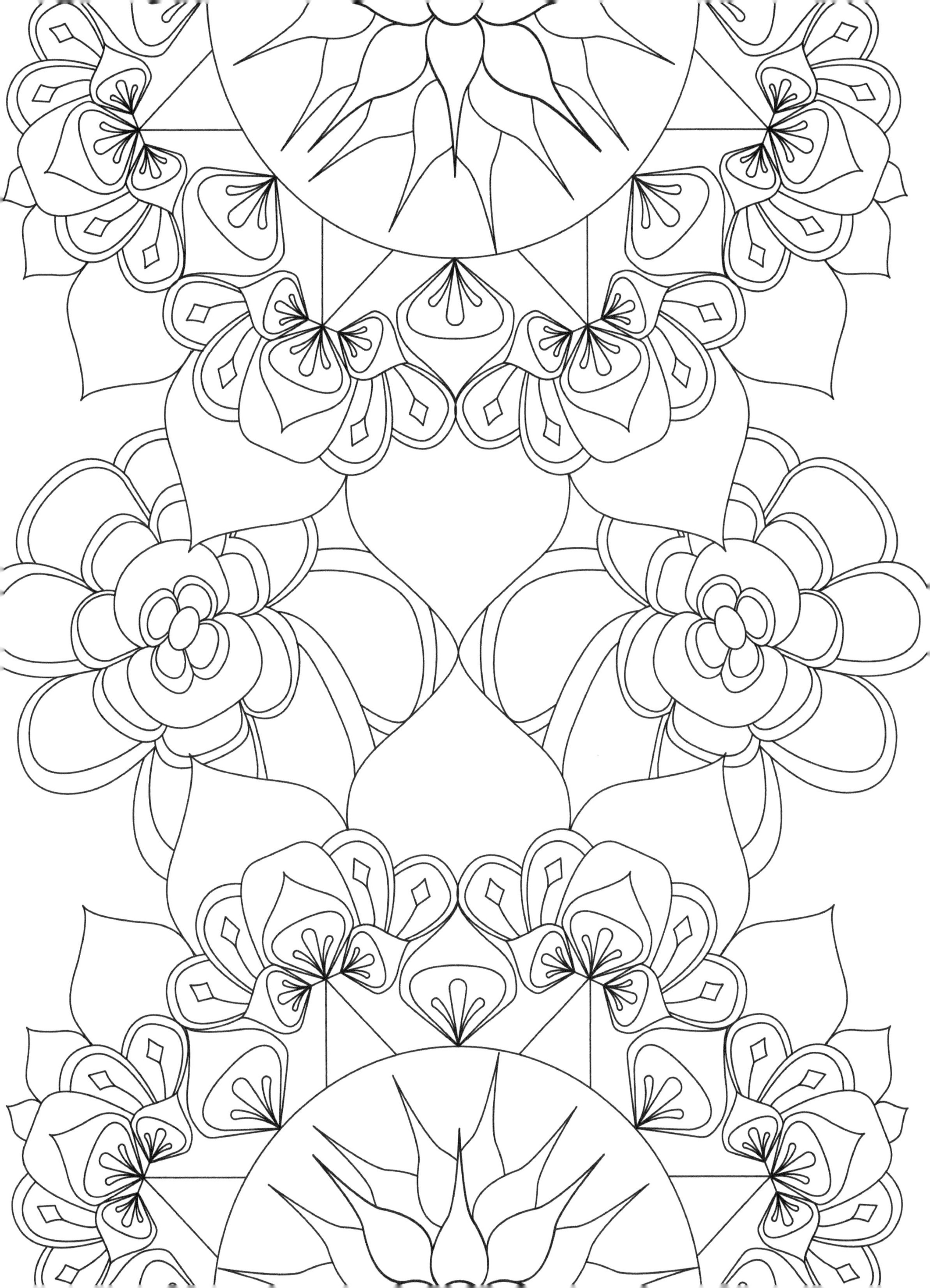

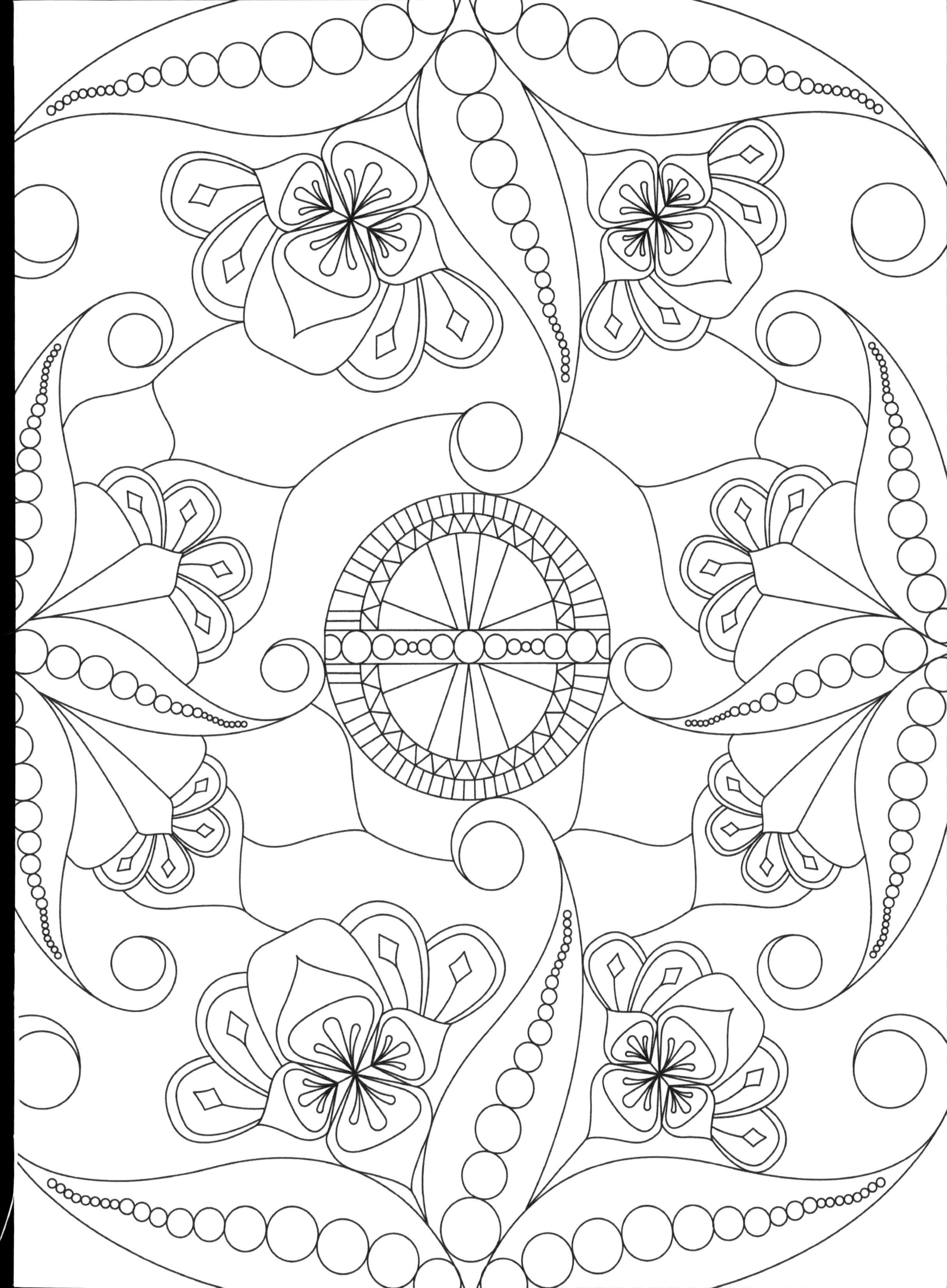

www.ingramcontent.com/pod-product-compliance
Lightning Source LLC
Chambersburg PA
CBHW060014210526
45170CB00018B/2939